Leveling Math Workstations in Grades K–2

In this book from bestselling author Dr. Nicki Newton, you'll learn how to level math workstations to engage K–2 students in meaningful, purposeful, rigorous practice. We know students don't learn at the same pace, so how do we take into account where they are and differentiate instruction? Dr. Nicki has the answers, showing how leveled workstations are key in the formative years, how they help students operate in their zone of proximal development and how we can use them to help students progress to higher levels of math achievement.

Topics include:

- Understanding the framework for leveled workstations
- Making sure workstations are rigorous and not just providing busy work
- Building your stations in key areas such as counting, numbers, place value, fluency and word problems
- Keeping students accountable, and knowing where they are in their learning trajectory

Each chapter offers specific examples, activities and tools. There is also a clear, step-by-step action plan to help you implement the ideas immediately in your own classroom.

Dr. Nicki Newton has been an educator for 30 years, working both nationally and internationally with students of all ages. She has worked on developing Math Workshop and Guided Math Institutes around the country; visit her website at www.drnickinewton.com. She is also an avid blogger (www.guided math.wordpress.com), tweeter (@drnickimath) and Pinterest pinner (www.pinterest.com/drnicki7).

Also Available from Dr. Nicki Newton
(www.routledge.com/eyeoneducation)

Daily Math Thinking Routines in Action:
Distributed Practices Across the Year

Mathematizing Your School:
Creating a Culture for Math Success
Co-authored by Janet Nuzzie

Math Problem Solving in Action:
Getting Students to Love Word Problems, Grades K–2

Math Problem Solving in Action:
Getting Students to Love Word Problems, Grades 3–5

Guided Math in Action:
Building Each Student's Mathematical Proficiency with
Small-Group Instruction

Math Workshop in Action:
Strategies for Grades K–5

Math Running Records in Action:
A Framework for Assessing Basic Fact Fluency in Grades K–5

Math Workstations in Action:
Powerful Possibilities for Engaged Learning in Grades 3–5

Leveling Math Workstations in Grades K–2

Strategies for Differentiated Practice

Dr. Nicki Newton

Routledge
Taylor & Francis Group

NEW YORK AND LONDON

First published 2019
by Routledge
52 Vanderbilt Avenue, New York, NY 10017

and by Routledge
2 Park Square, Milton Park, Abingdon, Oxon, OX14 4RN

Routledge is an imprint of the Taylor & Francis Group, an informa business

© 2019 Taylor & Francis

Library of Congress Cataloging-in-Publication Data
Names: Newton, Nicki, author.
Title: Leveling math workstations in grades K–2 : strategies for differentiated
    practice / Dr. Nicki Newton.
Description: New York : Routledge, 2019. | Includes bibliographical references.
Identifiers: LCCN 2018044615 (print) | LCCN 2018049964 (ebook) | ISBN
    9780429028601 (ebook) | ISBN 9780367137915 (hardback) | ISBN
    9780367137946 (pbk.) | ISBN 9780429028601 (ebook)
Subjects: LCSH: Mathematics—Study and teaching (Early childhood) |
    Mathematics—Study and teaching (Elementary) | Creative activities and seat
    work. | Activity programs in education. | Desks. | Teaching—Aids and devices.
Classification: LCC QA135.6 (ebook) | LCC QA135.6 .N4867 2019 (print) | DDC
    372.7/044—dc23
LC record available at https://lccn.loc.gov/2018044615

ISBN: 978-0-367-13791-5 (hbk)
ISBN: 978-0-367-13794-6 (pbk)
ISBN: 978-0-429-02860-1 (ebk)

Typeset in Sabon
by Apex CoVantage, LLC

I dedicate this book to Heidi Hayes Jacobs.

Contents

Preface

Teaching mathematics is about facilitating mathematical development. This means that you cannot get all learners to the same landmarks at the same time, in the same way, any more than you can get all toddlers to walk at the same time, in the same way! All you can do is provide a rich environment, turn your classroom into a mathematical community, and support the development of each child in the journey toward the horizon.

(Fosnot, 2007, p. 15)

I am excited to be writing this book. I have been wanting to write it for a long time. I am so excited by the work that people are doing with workstations. I just think we need to take it to the next level. We need to be more influenced by the work in literacy around workstations, meaning that in literacy, students work in their zone of proximal development. In math, it often seems like a free for all. We must get much more precise about how we structure and implement math workstations. In this book I am not trying to write about general math workstations. I want to make a very specific case for leveling math workstations so that all of our students are engaged in meaningful, purposeful, academically rigorous practice.

Chapter 1: Introduction

In this chapter we introduce leveled workstations, why we need them, when we do them, how they are different from regular math workstations, why they are important and how we use them to improve students' achievement.

Chapter 2: A Deeper Dive Into the Framework

In this chapter we look at the framework for leveled workstations. We look at the general framework of concrete, pictorial and abstract. We look at the need for rigor (Webb's DOK) and the intersection with Bloom's Taxonomy. We also look at the role of helping parents to help their students.

Chapter 3: Keeping Students Accountable

In this chapter we look at how to hold students accountable to the work they are practicing in the workstations. We discuss the different ways to assess students and how to know what they are doing and where they are on the learning trajectory.

Chapter 4: Counting Workstations

In this chapter we look at the role of the learning trajectories and how they should influence our set-up of counting workstations. Counting workstations should go way beyond setting up counting jars and counting bags. There are 20 levels of counting and we need stations that address the various needs of the students in our classrooms so that they are working on meaningful activities.

Chapter 5: Number Workstations

In this chapter we look at the role of the learning trajectories and how they should influence our set-up of subitizing and composing and decomposing workstations. These workstations should go way beyond matching dots with numbers on a card or doing a few number bonds. There are ten different levels for subitizing and five for composing and decomposing numbers and this should inform what, when and how these workstations are designed and implemented in the primary classroom.

Chapter 6: Place Value Workstations

There are 17 place value standards from kindergarten to second grade. They are intense and important because they lay the foundation for the rest of a student's mathematical career. If there are gaps, they don't close on their own. In fact, they widen and students fall deeper and deeper into the abyss as they go through the grades. So, providing scaffolded opportunities for students to really understand all of these place value ideas is crucial in the primary grades.

Chapter 7: Fluency Workstations

There are designated fluencies for each grade level. They are built on a hierarchy of knowing. The research calls this continuum "the sequence," "the phases of mastery" or the "levels of sophistication." We have to know what these are and design experiences so that students have a strong sense of number combinations and a confidence in working with whole numbers that they can carry into work with fractions, decimals and percents.

Chapter 8: Word Problem Workstations

There are four types of single-step word problems that students have to know, including 15 single-step types of word problems and five two-step types of word problems. This is a word problem hierarchy that every teacher needs to understand and scaffold the work around in their workstations. Although every state uses a schema-based approach to word problems, not every teacher knows this method of teaching word problems. If we know the levels then we can figure out where our students are, meet them there and take them to the next level.

Chapter 9: Action Planning

There always has to be a specific plan after you read a book. A plan helps you to go from being inspired to working that plan and using it to actually improve student achievement. Plans require that we think through the easy stuff, the challenging stuff, the beginning stuff and the long-term stuff. So, we are going to put dates and ideas together to get you moving and doing leveled workstations!

I have framed the leveled workstation around the CCSSM, Math TEKS and different Math State Standards:

National Governors Association Center for Best Practices, Council of Chief State School. (2010). Common Core State Standards for Mathematics.

19Tac Chapter 111. Texas Essential Knowledge and Skills for Mathematics. Retrieved On January, 2018 from http://ritter.tea.state.tx.us/rules/tac/chapter111/index.html

Reference

Fosnot, C. 2007. *Investigating Multiplication and Division: Getting Started with Contexts for Learning Mathematics, Grades 3–5*. Portsmouth, NH: Heinemann.

Acknowledgments

I love teaching teachers and I learned a lot of what I know from some great mentors at TC. Heidi Hayes Jacobs has been a monumental influence on my career. She mentored me and supported me and put me in contact with Bob, who published *Guided Math in Action*. Heidi taught me how to share my enthusiasm and to present with gusto and livelihood. I learned so much over the many years that I was her TA at Columbia. I am so grateful that I had the honor of working with her and learning from her every summer.

My family is my bedrock. I love them all and each and every one of them helps me in their own way. My brother and my sister, Marvin and Sharon, my Auntie Mary and my Uncle Bill and Auntie Lizzie, my many cousins, but especially Clinese Davis, who I talk to all the time. My assistants Brittany, Kiyana, Debbie and Gabby who make it all happen behind the scenes. I stand on the shoulders of my ancestors, my mom, my dad, my grandma and my grandpa. My friends are incredible; they support me, they believe in me and they want the best for me. My colleagues are amazing and the educators and students that I work with every day inspire me to do better, learn more and share it always.

1

Introduction

Workstations are purposeful opportunities to practice academically rigorous, engaging, standard-based "just right" math activities.

What Is a Workstation?

A workstation is a space for students to practice what they are learning and what they are supposed to know. They practice in different ways. Sometimes they practice by themselves, sometimes they practice with a partner and other times they practice in a small group. They can play various types of games as well as do different activities and projects. All of the activities should be meaningful, standards-based and rigorous. Workstations are not busy work. Workstations are not worksheets. Workstations are not supposed to be boring or frustrating. They are spaces to learn, to grow, to be challenged and to stretch. They are familiar. Students should never be at a workstation that they don't understand. Great workstations allow students to solidify their content knowledge and skills through purposeful practice in the student's zone of proximal development (Vygotsky, 1978). The purpose of the workstation is for students to make sense of the math that they are learning. It is a "constructive, interactive, problem solving" space with a variety of scaffolded experiences (Cobb, Yackel, & Wood, 1992, p. 99).

Knowledge is actively created or invented by the child, not passively received from the environment. This idea can be illustrated by the Piagetian position that mathematical ideas are made by children, not found like a pebble or accepted from others like a gift (Sinclair, in Steffe and Cobb, 1988 cited in Clements & Battista, 1990).

Leveled Workstations

Leveled workstations are about getting students to work in a scaffolded manner so that they can have a firm foundation and reach grade level standards. They are premised on the idea that you have to walk before you run.

They are premised on the idea that we teach children, not a pacing calendar. The pacing calendar is a guide to help ensure that we expose all children to a series of ideas throughout the year. We all know that not everyone learns at the same pace. Some students simply aren't ready for the current content. That doesn't mean that they won't be ready or get ready but it does mean that we need to make sure that everybody has a firm foundation in what they need in order to reach grade level standards. Some students are in the exact same place as the pacing calendar and others need a bit more practice before they get to those ideas. We need to take into account where all of the students are that we teach as we design workstations (see Figure 1.1).

"To effectively guide and support students in constructing the meaning of mathematical ideas, instruction must be derived from research-based descriptions of how students develop reasoning about particular mathematical topics" (Battista, 2016, p. 2).

Researchers warn us that because of "the enormous variability in young children's development" we mustn't set up arbitrary "fixed timeline[s] for children to reach each specific learning objective" (National Association for the Education of Young Children [NAEYC] & National Council of Teachers of Mathematics [NCTM], 2002, p. 5). It is irrational to expect students to learn seven different addition strategies in seven days. We don't expect students to do this in reading. We don't set arbitrary deadlines and say things like we have five days for everybody to get through reading level C. But in math, we do this and we need to stop. Leveled workstations allow students to work in their zone of proximal development so that they actually understand and learn the math we are trying to teach them. The NAEYC and NCTM joint document goes on to state that

> highly specific timetables for skill acquisition pose another serious threat, especially when accountability pressures are intense. They tend to focus teachers' attention on getting children to perform narrowly defined skills by a specified time, rather than on laying the conceptual groundwork that will serve children well in the long run.
>
> So everyone is rushed and learning is often "superficial" at best "at the expense of real understanding."

(NAEYC & NCTM)

Leveled workstations are about giving students the opportunity and the time needed to learn and own the mathematical ideas they are working with. In order to level, we have to be aware of the different developmental stages of learning a concept. We need to know what came before the standard, what came after the standard and what the microprogressions are within the standard.

Figure 1.1 Examples of Workstations

A Look in Two Classrooms	
Mrs. L	Mrs. C
Fluency Station: Everybody is playing a make 10 game. Numbers: All the students are working on the same 3 counting jars.	Fluency Station: Students are working on different activities. Mark and Claire are playing a board game where they are adding within 5. They can use their counters to help scaffold their thinking. Luke and Tyler are playing a make 10 game card game.
Word Problems: Everybody is working on 1 word problem. Some students are flying through it and others don't know what is happening.	Numbers: There are different levels of counting jars. Some students are counting within 5, others within 10 and some above 10. Word Problems: Tim and Annie are working on level 5 word problems, while Mark and Kelly are working on level 7 word problems.

Why Do It?

Math is hierarchical. We can't just pass steps. If we do, we skip the foundational pieces that hold together the whole thing. As educators we have to take seriously the research-based learning trajectories that should inform our curriculum, pedagogy and assessment. We have to know what is expected and when. We need to understand how to assess the math that our students know and what the nuances of the assessment are. We need to let that inform our curriculum and our pedagogy. Too often, people will say to me, "my students can't do 'this'" and then when I ask for further clarification they can't give it. We all need to learn the trajectories.

Teachers must "have an understanding of the general stages that students pass through in acquiring the concepts and procedures in the domain, the processes that are used to solve different problems at each stage, and the nature of the knowledge that underlies these processes." (Carpenter & Fennema, 1991, p. 11).

Somewhere there is a disconnect between what researchers know and what teachers know. We have to all get better at bridging that if we are going to improve student achievement. The thing is that if we don't know where we are going then we aren't very likely to get there. So we must know better so that we can do better. Furthermore, if everyone does the same thing at the same time, then we have some students who are bored and others who are frustrated. So we do leveled workstations so that everyone is working on their "just right" activities.

When?

We need to level workstations from the beginning. When we are setting up our counting workstations we should be conscientious that there are 20 levels of counting. Where are our students? How does that impact how we set up different types of learning activities for them? Should everybody be doing the same counting activities? Should everybody be doing the same subitizing activities when we know there are 10 levels of subitizing? What about place value? Some second graders are still struggling with first grade place value understandings, so why don't we get them to understand the first steps before we move them along? We have to start thinking about how to do this. We have students learning how "to bridge 10" when they don't even know how "to make 10." Let's start leveling workstations (independent practice) from the beginning.

How?

Assessment is the key to leveling workstations. We have to know where students are so we can decide where and how we need to take them next on their learning journey. For example, in kindergarten, there are 20 levels of counting. If we know what level our students are then we can set up counting activities that are appropriate for practice. Kayla could be at a level 6 where she is working on counting objects within 5 and Maria could be working at a level 8 where she is working on counting objects within 10. The students could even be working on the same type of activity but with different numbers. Maybe they are doing counting boards where they have to put that many counters on the board and it is scaffolded to their levels.

Let's take a first grade example. There are some students who still don't get K place value ideas. They don't understand the concept of a ten and a one. In first grade students start working with numbers within 120. So, if we have a place value center set up for students to work on throughout the year, when they actually get to place value, they will be ready because they have been reviewing the K concepts all year. In second grade, there are some first graders who are very shaky on place value. Let's take the idea of adding two two-digit numbers. Some students are still struggling with the first grade standard of adding a one-digit number and a two-digit number. So, a place value workstation in second grade would have some K activities and some first grade activities and the second grade activities as introduced.

Which Stations Should Be Leveled?

I always tell teachers that less is more. When we have too many stations it becomes overwhelming for everybody involved. So, we should prioritize the priority standards and make sure that the majority of the time that we spend in workstations is devoted to fostering, developing and securing those big ideas and skills that we need students to know in that grade. In kindergarten, numbers and counting and geometry are great stations to start with and level throughout the year. In first grade, students are still working with numbers and counting, but also place value, fluency and word problems are introduced as stations. In second grade, the focus is on fluency, place value and word problems. Throughout the year there should be a station that rotates every unit, that works on the big ideas of the current unit of study and it could be leveled (for example, time in second grade).

A Quick Overview of When Students Do Workstations

Workstations can be done as part of a math workshop or they can be done as part of a regular math program that isn't in a workshop format. Either way, the purpose of math workstations is for the students to have an opportunity to do purposeful, meaningful, independent practice. I highly encourage people to do a Math Workshop format. I have written a book on Math Workshop (which details all aspects). In a Math Workshop (see Figure 1.2) there are three parts.

Opening

- Energizers and Routines
- Problem Solving
- Mini-Lesson

Student Activity

- Math Workstations
- Guided Math Groups

Debrief

- Discussion
- Exit Slip
- Mathematician's Chair Share

Figure 1.2 Workshop Model Overview

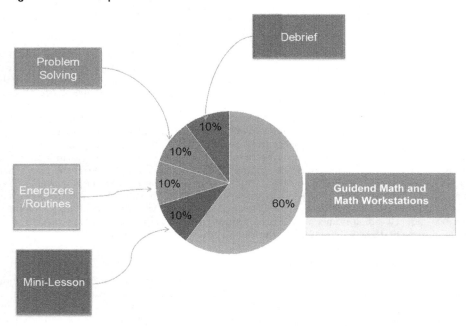

Figure 1.3 Research on Early Childhood Math

Researcher	Research	Big Ideas	How Does This Research Inform Our Practice?
Clements, D. H., & Sarama, J. (2009). *Learning and Teaching Early Math: The Learning Trajectories Approach.* New York: Routledge.	Learning trajectories research.	There is a developmental landscape for learning math.	Does the teaching and learning of math at your school reflect the developmental learning trajectories?
Cameron, A., Hersch, S., & Fosnot, C. 2004. *Fostering Children's Mathematical Development: The Landscape of Learning.* Canada: Pearson Education.	In order to effectively differentiate instruction, everybody at all grade levels needs to know the landscapes of learning.	"The metaphor of a landscape evokes a picture of a learning terrain through which pre-kindergartners, and first, second, and third graders move in meandering or direct ways as they develop number sense, addition, and subtraction."	Has your school done vertical planning where everyone knows the landscape of learning from K–2? How is the idea of a landscape of learning reflected in your workstations?
Battista, M. (2016). *Reasoning and Sense Making in the Mathematics Classroom: Pre-K–Grade 2,* pp. 27–59. Reston, VA: National Council of Teachers of Mathematics.	Concrete rather than abstract learning.	"If instruction is too abstract for students' current states of understanding, they will not be able to make the appropriate jump in personal sense making" (p. 15).	In what ways do your current workstations assess the personal sense making of concepts that students are engaging in?
Bruner, J. (1979). *On Knowing: Essays for the Left Hand.* Cambridge, MA: Belknap Press. (Original work published in 1962).	The role of discovery in student learning.	"The virtues of encouraging discovery are of two kinds. In the first place, the child will make what he learns his own, will fit his discovery into the interior world of culture that he creates for himself. Equally important, discovery and the sense of confidence it provides is the proper reward for learning" (pp. 123–124).	In what ways do your current workstations allow for the discovery of concepts?
Steffe, Leslie P. & D'Ambrosio B. (1995) Toward a Working Model of Constructivist Teaching: A Reaction to Simon. *Journal for Research in Mathematics Education,* 26, 146–159. Cobb, P., Wood, T., & Yackel, E. (1990). Classrooms as Learning Environments for Teachers and Researchers. In R. B. Davis, C. A. Maher, & N. Noddings (Eds.), Constructivist views on the teaching and learning of mathematics. *Journal for Research in Mathematics Education,* Monograph Number 4, 125–146. Reston, VA: National Council of Teachers of Mathematics.	Instructional tasks must be based on where students are currently working (Steffe & D'Ambrosio, 1995).	Workstations should be "grounded in detailed analyses of children's mathematical experiences and the processes by which they construct mathematical knowledge" (Cobb, Wood, & Yackel, 1990, p. 130).	Are your current workstations evidence-based?

⚷ Key Points

- Leveled Workstations
- Hierarchical Progressions
- Start in K
- Level Fluency, Place Value and Word Problems

Summary

Leveled workstations are important so that students can practice in their zone of proximal development (see Figure 1.3). We must all learn the continuums for primary content and align our instructional activities with them. Even in kindergarten, we need to know the nuances in the counting continuum, given that there are 20 levels. It is important to level the priority standard workstations so that students can practice throughout the year (closing gaps) and leave having achieved the grade level standard.

Reflection Questions

1. How well would you say that the people on your grade level know the developmental learning continuums for counting, numbers, place value, basic fact fluency and word problems?
2. What have you learned from this chapter?
3. How will you use what you have learned from this chapter?

References

Battista, M. (2016). *Reasoning and Sense Making in the Mathematics Classroom: Pre-K–Grade 2*. Reston, VA: National Council of Teachers of Mathematics, pp. 27–59.

Carpenter, T. P. & Fennema, E. (1991). Research and Cognitively Guided Instruction. In E. Fennema, T. P. Carpenter, & S. J. Lamon (Eds.), *Integrating Research on Teaching and Learning Mathematics*. Albany, NY: State University of New York Press, pp. 1–16.

Cobb, P., Yackel, E., & Wood, T. (1992). Interaction and Learning in Mathematics Classroom Situations. *Educational Studies in Mathematics*, 23(1), 99–122.

NAEYC/NCTM—National Association for the Education of Young Children and the National Council of Teachers of Mathematics (2002/2010). *Early Childhood Mathematics: Promoting Good Beginnings*. Joint position paper adopted in 2002, updated in 2010. http://www.naeyc.org/files/naeyc/file/positions/psmath.pdf. January 30, 2019.

Vygotsky, L. S. (1978). *Mind in Society: The Development of Higher Psychological Processes*. Cambridge, MA: Harvard University Press.

2

A Deeper Dive Into the Framework

Getting started is simple! Just start. Start small but START!

Big Ideas/Enduring Understandings/Essential Questions

It is important that teachers consider and explore the big ideas of learning for each workstation. Based on the big ideas, educators must then consider what are the best learning activities to get the students to where they need to be. What are the essential questions for the workstation? Heidi Hayes Jacobs says that "essential questions are the Velcro of any unit" (personal communication). I would say that they are also the Velcro of a workstation. It is too easy to just put busy work in workstations or pretty work or cut and paste activities. We have to consider the big ideas of the station and then create learning experiences based on the big ideas, the enduring understandings and the essential questions.

The Ontario Ministry of Education states that

> the big ideas also act as a "lens" for: Making instructional decisions; identifying prior learning; looking at students' thinking and understanding in relation to the mathematical concepts addressed in the curriculum; collecting observations and making anecdotal records; providing feedback to students; determining next steps; communicating concepts and providing feedback on student's achievement to parents.
>
> (p. 4)

Teachers must understand the key ideas that their students need to know, the skills that they must be able to do and how these concepts connect with what came before and what comes next (Ma, 1999). Teachers need to not only know what the concepts are but how to best teach them to the students. What are the learning trajectories required to fully understand the concepts and be able to do the math? What does the journey look like? What could it look like? What should it look like? For whom, when and where?

Concrete/Pictorial/Abstract Cycle of Engagement

For example, at the concrete level students might be working on Play-Doh mats but the numbers on the mats change depending on the number range of the station. At the pictorial level, students might be expected to roll and draw, but again it is aligned with the number range at the workstation. Finally, at the abstract level, students might play a board game at the station but the numbers would be different at each level (see Figure 2.1).

During the cycle of engagement, students work with various concrete materials to understand the basic concept and then work with the concepts further through representations and finally symbolic representations. The idea is that the students have several opportunities to unpack ideas and strategies using this cycle,

> a continual exposure to enactment-iconic-symbolic cycle leads to a formation of links among the representations into a collective structure. It is when the mathematical symbol becomes the dominate representation in this collective structure that the state of learned is reached.
>
> (Hui, Lee, & Koay, 2017, p. 5)

This is a "tailored sequence" that is shaped around the student's developmental progression of the ideas and skills. Gattegno stated that "the teaching was subordinated by the learning (1987)." Put simply,

Figure 2.1 Example of Concrete, Pictorial and Abstract Activity

Number Bracelets		
This is an activity that can be used across various counting stations. The number changes but the activity stays the same.		
Concrete Activity	Pictorial Activity	Abstract Activity
	Use your number bracelet. Show the 2 ways to make 7 on your bracelet! Draw it! | 3 + 4	5 + 2 | |---|---| | | | *Students should have opportunities to interpret an expression as well as opportunities to create their own expressions. In this particular activity they are working from the concrete to the pictorial. They are also working with the abstract because they have to interpret the expression.	Use your number bracelet. Find 2 ways to make 7, draw it and record it on the sheet! | __ + __ | __ + __ | |---|---| | | |

this means that we don't just teach page 99 because it is November 8th. Where are the students? What are the gaps that need to be addressed so they understand the concepts on page 99? What scaffolding needs to take place for students to fully grasp page 99? Even when students are right and ready for page 99, many times they need more concept-building time than is allotted in the book. We all know that you don't learn doubles on November 8th, doubles plus 1 on November 9th and doubles plus 2 on November 10th! The question is what are we doing with that knowledge that is in the best interest of the students? I would argue that leveled workstations allow us to address this issue in a meaningful way.

Similar Activities/Different Number Ranges

Many times the activity doesn't change; it is just modified to be practiced at the level of the student. This is an important idea when creating workstations. You want variety but you also want familiarity. Students should have several games to choose from but they should also have games that they recognize and know how to play. Remember that it is important that students always understand what they are doing when they go to a workstation. They should never be at a workstation where they don't know how to do the task. Having familiar activities facilitates the process of being able to go to a workstation and get started and be on task. That being said, there should be a variety of activities for students to practice the math. The structure could be the same but the details could be different, meaning that clip cards are a basic structure for workstations. They can be used in counting, fluency, workstations and word problems. The picture and the layout can all change (see Figure 2.2).

Scaffolded to Unscaffolded Activities

Throughout the various workstations, there should be a conscious effort to think about scaffolding. Scaffolding is a temporary structure that allows access to the task.

Anghilieri (2006) points out that scaffolding is about responsive guidance:

> Marked changes from traditional teaching approaches are needed as the role of the teacher changes from "showing and telling" to responsive guidance in developing pupils' own thinking. This guidance requires a range of support for pupils' thought constructions, in a way that develops individual thinking as well as leading to the generation of mathematically valid understandings.

In terms of leveled math workstations, responsive guidance is about teachers responding to students' stages of understanding through intentional learning opportunities and practice. Teachers

Figure 2.2 Examples of Clip Cards

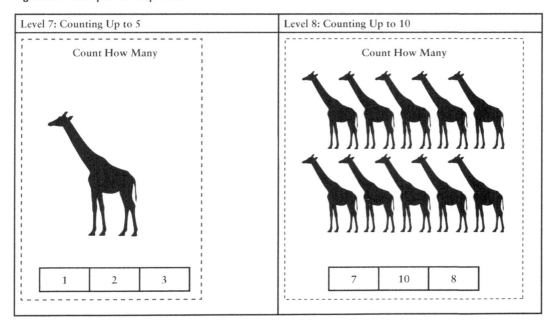

scaffold the learning landscapes through leveled activities that meet the specific needs of individual students. Let's think about it across math topics. For example, in the counting workstation, students in Station C are working on counting numbers within 5. So, when they start, they might be counting numbers up to 5 on a template that is scaffolded with the dots. However, as they continue to practice counting up to 5, the scaffold is removed and they have to count a set without any scaffolding (see Figure 2.3).

Figure 2.3 Examples of Scaffolding

Rigor Inventory

It is really important that teachers talk about the level of rigor in the activities that the students are doing in the workstations. It is important that we honestly evaluate if the activities are a level 1 or a level 2 or 3. We need to think about how we work within these levels across workstations. Oftentimes, if we don't discuss and evaluate the workstations, many of the workstations are level 1. So having conversations about criteria, about what makes a workstation what level, allows everyone to raise the rigor of the station and to see the difference in levels. Oftentimes, it is a small tweak that makes a big difference in the rigor level in a station. We are also always thinking about the intersection between Bloom (1956) and Webb (2002). Hess (2004) gives a framework to look at how these intersect. Good workstations don't just happen; they are planned for and then evaluated and adjusted. A good workstation is a working curriculum space subject to change whenever needed.

It is important to have a variety of activities in the workstations. There should be some level 1, some level 2 and some level 3 activities. Too often there are only level 1 activities. It is important to remember that what is a level 3 activity in one grade can be a level 1 activity in another. Here is an example of what that might look like (see Figure 2.4).

Figure 2.4 Rigor

Rigor Inventory: Going From Good to Great!		
DOK Level 1 Recall	DOK Level 2 Skill	DOK Level 3 Strategic Thinking
Find the number 12 on the number line.	Put the numbers in order and underline the number 12.	Which one of these number lines is correct? Explain your thinking.
John had 3 marbles. Mike had 5. How many did they have altogether?	John had some marbles. Mike had 5. Together they have 8. How many does John have?	Write a word problem where the answer is 8 marbles.
Find the sum of 25 + 39.	Make 64 ___ + ___ = 64 ___ – ___ = 64	Add 25 + 39 in two different ways. Explain each strategy. Discuss which one is more efficient and why.

Here are some questions to ask during a rigor inventory (see Figure 2.5). I didn't include level 4 here because not very many workstations are going to have level 4 activities. A level 4 activity would be a project that took time and had several phases.

Figure 2.5 DOK

DOK Level 1 Recall and Reproduce	DOK Level 2 Use Skills	DOK Level 3 Think Strategically and Reasonably: Explain How and Why
Are they following a procedure?	Are they using a concept to do something?	Do they have to prove or justify their thinking?
Do they simply have to recall something to complete the activity?	Do they have to explain their thinking? Are they using models and diagrams to explain their thinking?	Do they have to describe, compare and contrast strategies?
Is it a single step?	Is it multiple steps?	Is it an open-ended question where students have to make their own problems?

Based on Webb (2002).

Figure 2.6 Research on Teaching Primary Math

Researcher	Research	Big Ideas	How Does This Research Inform Our Practice?
Anghileri, J. (2006). Scaffolding Practices that Enhance Mathematics. *Journal of Math Teacher Education, 9*(1), 33–52.	Three levels of scaffolding.	Three-level hierarchy of scaffolding practices that specifically support mathematics learning: Level 1: Environmental provisions (classroom organization, artefacts such as blocks). Level 2: Explaining, reviewing and restructuring. Level 3: Developing conceptual thinking.	Are you scaffolding at all three levels? Do your workstations reflect carefully planned scaffolding?
National Association for the Education of Young Children and National Council of Teachers of Mathematics (2002). *Early Childhood Mathematics: Promoting Good Beginnings.*	It is important to plan activities for individuals where they are along the learning path.	It is important to know and be informed by the research on how children learn. For certain topics in math, researchers have written about "a developmental continuum or learning path—a sequence indicating how particular concepts and skills build on others" (pp. 44, 47, 48). If we are going to reach all learners we need to understand, "that some children will grasp a concept earlier and others somewhat later. Expecting and planning for such individual variation are always important" (p. 7).	In what ways are you consistently and specifically "expecting and planning for individual variation" around the priority standards throughout the year in your math workstations?
Ketterlin-Geller, L. R., Chard, D. J., & Fien, H. (2008). Making Connections in Mathematics: Conceptual Mathematics Intervention for Low-performing Students. *Remedial and Special Education, 29*(1), 33–45. Flores, M. M. (2010). Using the Concrete-representational-abstract Sequence to Teacher Subtraction with Regrouping to Students at Risk for Failure. *Remedial and Special Education, 31*(3), 195–207.	CRA is important for struggling learners as well as typical learners.	Researchers have found that "a graduated instructional sequence that proceeds from concrete to representational to abstract (CRA) benefits struggling students" (Ketterlin-Geller, Chard, & Fien, 2008, p. 35; Flores, 2010; Butler et al, 2003; Maccini & Hughes, 2000).	Where is there evidence that you use the CRA cycle for the teaching and learning of priority concepts and skills in the math workstations?

(Continued)

Figure 2.6 Continued

Researcher	Research	Big Ideas	How Does This Research Inform Our Practice?
Butler, F. M., Miller, S. P., Crehan, K., Babbit, B., & Pierce, T. (2003). Fraction Instruction for Students with Mathematics Disabilities: Comparing Two Teaching Sequences. *Learning Disabilities Research and Practice*, 18, 99–111. Maccini, P. & Hughes, C. A. (2000). Effects of a Problem-solving Strategy on the Introductory Algebra Performance of Secondary Students with Learning Disabilities. *Learning Disabilities Research and Practice*, 15(1), 10–21.			
Robert Kaplinsky (2018) https://robertkaplinsky.com/tag/depth-of-knowledge-dok/	DOK is about deep thinking. It is easy to increase the rigor of a task by a simple change.	Kaplinsky has started a website that has examples of the math standards showing different levels of tasks.	Have you done a rigor check in your workstations? What are the levels of activities? Are they varied?
Small, M. (2012). *Good Questions: Great Ways to Differentiate Math Instructions*. New York: Teachers College, Columbia University.	Open questions challenge students to think and reason more deeply than closed questions.	Marian Small has done a lot of work on asking good questions. She has written several books on questioning and using open tasks. For example, she says to ask questions and tasks like: Show 9 in as many ways as you can. How are the numbers 10 and 15 alike? How are they different? The answer is 39, what is the question?	Do you make sure that your workstations have both open and closed tasks?

Key Points

- Concrete/Pictorial/Abstract Cycle of Engagement
- Scaffolded to Unscaffolded Activities
- Rigor Inventory

Summary

One of the main premises of the workstations is that everybody is working toward grade level standards all year. We are all going to get there, just maybe not at the same time. People are uncomfortable with that, and worried about what happens if John doesn't know it by the end of the chapter test. This is fair given the realities of school-pacing calendars but we have to think about what we are doing in schools.

Who says that everybody has to be on the same page at the same time? We just don't do this in reading! We understand that students are reading at different levels and we support, promote, encourage and scaffold grade level achievement but we don't set these arbitrary deadlines. We absolutely need a paradigm shift. Somebody has got to stand up and ask, "how do we do this differently?" What does it look like if we actually teach the kids and not just the textbook? If we are on page 205 and some kids are on page 105, others on page 205 and some on page 305, what do we do? How do we reach everyone? Isn't that their right as a student in a place called school where we are supposed to be teaching each and every one of them? I believe that well thought-out workstations are part of the solution to this pressing question.

Workstations have to be rigorous. They can't just be busy work. They can't just be low-level activities. They have to be engaging, standards-based and thinking activities (see Figure 2.6). They shouldn't be worksheets but students must record their thinking so we know what they are doing. In order to plan for the appropriate types of activities in workstations we must know the continuums for math and then we must know where the students are along those continuums.

Reflection Questions

1. How prevalent is the cycle of concrete, pictorial and abstract in your teaching?
2. Do you consider the balance of scaffolded and unscaffolded activities when setting up student work?
3. Do you ever analyze the level of rigor in the lessons you are teaching and the activities that you are doing?

References

Bloom, B. S. (1956). *Taxonomy of Educational Objectives, Handbook 1: Cognitive Domain*. New York: Addison Wesley Longman, Inc.

Gattegno, C. (1987). *What We Owe Children: The Subordination of Teaching to Learning*. New York: Educational Solutions Worldwide Inc.

Hess, K. (2004). *Applying Webb's Depth-of-Knowledge Levels in Reading*. [online]. www.nciea.org

Hui, C. S., Lee, N. H. & Koay, P. L. (2017). Teaching and Learning with Concrete-Pictorial-Abstract Sequence—A Proposed Model. *The Mathematics Educator*, 17(1–2), 1–28.

Ma, L. (1999). *Knowing and Teaching Elementary Mathematics: Teachers' Understanding of Fundamental Mathematics in China and the United States*. Mahwah, NJ: Lawrence Erlbaum.

Webb, N. (2002). *Depth-of-Knowledge levels for four content areas*. Retrieved from the web pdf September 2, 2017.

3

Keeping Students Accountable

If it's not on the sheet, it might have never happened!

Recording Sheets

The important thing about workstations is that students have to be accountable to the activities and games that they are engaging in. There should be recording sheets for almost everything that students do. Some activities just don't have recording sheets but the teacher can tell the students not to clean up, for example, the Play-Doh workstations, until she checks them. Or, students can take pictures of their work with iPads or their tablets. Or, the teacher can look at the workstations when he or she is not scheduled in a guided math station. There are many ways to go about making sure that students are doing the work they are supposed to do in the workstations and keeping track of that work. Here are a few guiding questions:

- How do I know if my students understand the concept?
- What is the evidence that they are fluent with the skill?
- How do I measure that growth overtime?
- What pieces of evidence will I collect that prove the student is making progress?

Teachers should have several different systems for keeping track of what is happening in the workstations (see Figure 3.1). The first really important system is that all students should have workstation folders that they keep at their desk or in a workstation folder area. The folders can be divided into a green dot and a red dot side. On the green dot side is the work that is currently being done. It is a work in progress. The red dot side means that the work has been completed. How these are filed depends on teacher preference. Student workstation recording sheets go in these folders. Also, in these folders are workstation reflection sheets and entrance and exit slips.

Self-Tracking Sheets and Self-Checking

It is important that students keep track of the work they have done in the workstation. Researchers have found that self-regulation strategies whereby students monitor, manage, record, observe, reflect on, assess and evaluate their own work can be very effective (Kingsdorf, Krawec, & Gritter, 2016).

There are different ways to do this. There can be a list of the activities that students are expected to accomplish in that workstation and as students accomplish the work, they check it off (see Figures 3.2 and 3.3).

It is also important that students can self-correct the work they do. In most, if not all cases, there should be a way for students to check their work by looking up the answer and comparing it with what they thought was the answer. Sometimes, the answer key is looked at after the game is done, or sometimes the answer key is checked by the partner as the game is taking place.

> "*Modifying tasks to include a* self-correcting *element can provide further feedback that supports pupils' autonomous learning, not only in finding a solution, but also in reflecting on the processes involved in such a solution*" (Anghileri, 2006, p. 7).

Figure 3.1 Keeping Track

Folder	Recording Sheet	Entrance/Exit Slips
I finished! / I am still working on this.	(Notice the use of the academic language in this recording sheet) Partner 1 / Partner 2 I rolled ___ / I rolled ___ ___ is greater than ___ ___ ◯ ___ Pick a number: _____ Write the word form: Base ten sketch / Expand it: Plot it on a number line: • Plot a number greater than your number. • Plot a number smaller than your number. • Compare the numbers with symbols.	Today I learned: I think adding within 100 is _____ easy or tricky Here are two ways to add 26 + 59: Way 1 / Way 2

Figure 3.2 Student Workstation Checklist

Place Value Exploring Tens and Ones Workstation Checklist		
Concrete Activities Pick Three	**Pictorial Activities Pick Three**	**Abstract Activities Pick Three**
Rekenrek Make and Show	Board Game See it, Say it, Draw it	Spinner: Roll it, Chart it, Sketch it, Find it
Spin it and Show it with Ten Frame	Spin it and Show it with Ten Frame	Spin it and Find it on the Hundred Grid
Spin it and Show it with Base Ten Blocks	Spin it and Show it with Base Ten Blocks	Base Ten Riddles
Bean Stick Toolkit	Spinner: Roll it, Chart it, Sketch it, Find it	Number Concentration

Digital Links:
http://ewnumbergrid.herokuapp.com/
http://www.mathlearningcenter.org/web-apps/number-pieces/
http://www.abcya.com/base_ten_bingo.htm
http://www.fuelthebrain.com/games/base-ten/

Figure 3.3 Student Workstation Reflection Sheet

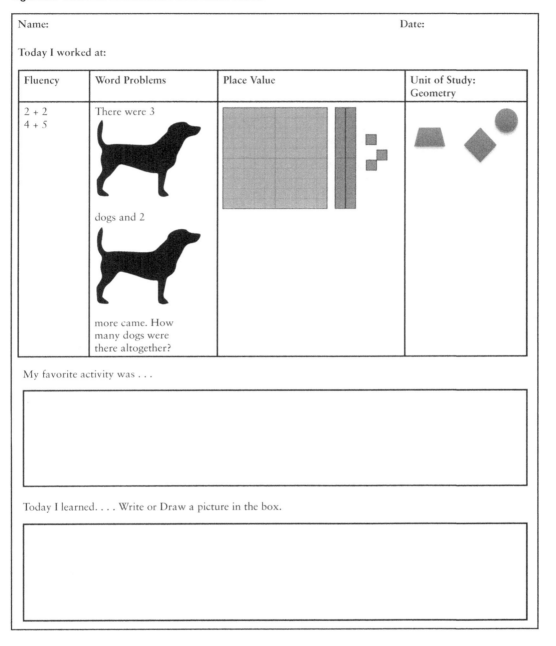

Fluency	Word Problems	Place Value	Unit of Study: Geometry
2 + 2 4 + 5	There were 3 dogs and 2 more came. How many dogs were there altogether?		

My favorite activity was . . .

Today I learned. . . . Write or Draw a picture in the box.

Keeping Students Accountable to the Academic Language

Students should be using the language appropriate to the content that they are working on. To help students do this, teachers should give them the vocabulary and the phraseology of what they are doing. For example, in the place value workstation, if the students were playing a compare game they might have this on a sentence strip (see Figures 3.4 and 3.5).

"Students are involved not only in discovery and invention but in a social discourse involving explanation, negotiation, sharing and evaluation" (Kamii & Lewis, 1990).

Figure 3.4 Language Stems

I rolled a _____ and my partner rolled a _____. _____ is greater than _____.

There might also be a vocabulary poster in the workstation.

Figure 3.5 Vocabulary Poster

Words we use when comparing numbers		
Greater than	>	7 > 8
Less than	<	1 < 10
Equal to	=	7 = 7

Anecdotals

Teachers should also keep anecdotal records of students' work in workstations. These are done when the teacher is walking around and observing what is happening in the workstation. Sometimes, the teacher sits in the workstation and interviews the group about what they are doing or the partners about the game they are playing or the individual students. Moreover, math workstations should be discussed when teachers are conferring with students about their math achievement. There are many ways to keep anecdotals. There is no one right way. Every teacher has to use a system that works for them (see Figure 3.6).

Figure 3.6 Examples of Anecdotals

Class Sheet	Post-It Note Folder (Quick Anecdotals)
Tom / Mary / Sue / Brit Joe / Rafael / Kiyana / Greg Jamal / Mike / Mason / Marven Shakhira / Susana / Kelly / Marta	

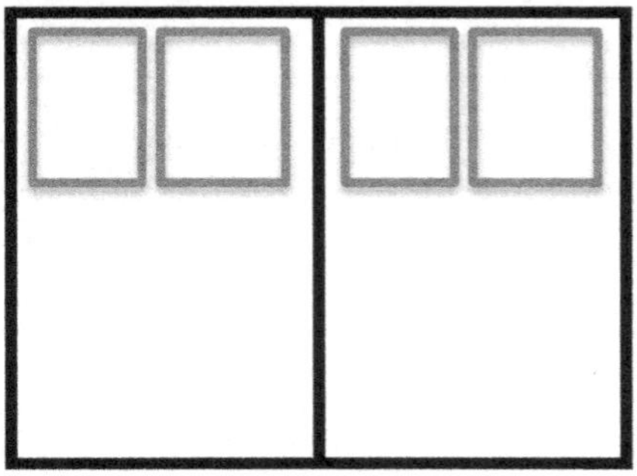

Keeping Track of It All

Teachers want to have individual data about the workstations along with class data about the workstation and it is also good to look at grade data about the workstations (see Figure 3.7). Some workstations should be used throughout the grade level so that there is consistency across the grade in terms of the content that students are exposed to. Grade level teachers should decide what is a mandated shared workstation and then what is free choice. Everybody will have the basics and then they can add on to that as they choose. For example, it is important to be able to discuss fluency across different data sets and how different activities are impacting student achievement levels, so having agreed-upon practice experiences benefits everyone in the grade.

Figure 3.7 Examples of Notes

Notes on the Individual Student	Notes on the Group	Notes About the Class
Juan Carlos has learned his doubles. I watched him in the workstation today and he is doing it fluently. Possibly move him on to doubles plus 1.	Today in Guided Math Group 3, the students were all struggling with adding 10 on the hundreds grid. Mike seems to get it better than the others but I think we need to go back to doing more concrete work. Do with base ten blocks again next time.	Today during the What Doesn't Belong routine, many of them were confused about the irregular hexagons.

Helping Parents/Guardians Help Their Children

In thinking about the leveling of workstations it is important that there is a parent/guardian connection. Parents/guardians need to know what the landscape of learning looks like and where their child is on that landscape. Parents/guardians need to know what is the next step and how they can best help their child to achieve that. Schools need to make handouts, booklets and handbooks of the landscapes with videos so that parents and guardians have the tools that they need to help their children. Schooling has changed and parents/guardians need help to understand many of the different ways that we are now teaching math (see Figure 3.8).

Figure 3.8 Parents/Guardians Communication

Newsletter	Chapter Update	Grade Level Handbook
The newsletter is a general conversation about the upcoming quarter. It should focus on the specific priority standards being taught during that quarter/semester/grading period and how parents/guardians might help.	During the current chapter of study, teachers should send home a chapter update that talks about what students are learning and how parents/guardians can reinforce those concepts at home.	The grade level handbook should have the standards for the grade unpacked with pictorial representations so parents/guardians know exactly what is expected. There should be a special emphasis on the priority standards.

Figure 3.9 Research on Early Childhood Math

Researcher	Research	Big Ideas	How Does This Research Inform Our Practice?
Marzano, R. retrieved on September 8, 2018 from www.ascd.org/publications/educational-leadership/dec09/vol67/num04/When-Students-Track-Their-Progress.aspx#fn1	Visually tracking student data has profound effects on teacher effectiveness and student achievement.	"For example, Fuchs and Fuchs (1986) found that providing teachers with graphic displays of students' scores on formative assessments was associated with a 26 percentile point gain in achievement." "On average, the practice of having students track their own progress was associated with a 32 percentile point gain in their achievement."	In what ways do you use visual data to track student work? In what ways do you have the students use visual data to track their work? How do you relate this data to the workstations?
Capraro, R. M., Capraro, M. M., & Rupley, W. H. (2010). Semantics and Syntax: A Theoretical Model for How Students May Build Mathematical Misunderstandings. *Journal of Mathematics Education*, 3(2), 58–66. doi:http://dx.doi.org/10.1080/02702710060642467 Davis, F. B. (1968). Research in Comprehension in Reading. *Reading Research Quarterly*, 3, 499–545. —. 1972. Psychometric Research on Comprehension in Reading. *Reading Research Quarterly*, 7(4), 628–678. doi:http://dx.doi.org/10.2307/747108 Espin, C. A. & Foegen, A. (1996). Validity of General Outcome Measures for Predicting Secondary Students' Performance on Content-Area Tasks. *Exceptional Children*, 62, 497–514. Fisher, D. & Frey, N. (2008). *Word Wise and Content Rich, Grades 7–12: Five Essential Steps to Teaching Academic Vocabulary*. Portsmouth, NH: Heinemann. Fitzgerald, J. & Graves, M. F. (2005). Reading Supports for All. *Educational Leadership*, 62(4), 68–71. Kotsopoulos, D. (2007). Mathematics Discourse: "It's Like Hearing a Foreign Language." *Mathematics Teacher*, 101(4), 301–305. Nagy, W. E. (1988). *Teaching Vocabulary to Improve Reading Comprehension*. Newark, DE: International Reading Association.	Language is key to students' conceptual understanding of mathematics.	Vocabulary impacts comprehension and conceptual understanding (Davis, 1968; Fitzgerald & Graves, 2005; Nagy, 1988; Espin & Foegen, 1996; Capraro, Capraro, & Rupley, 2010; Kotsopoulous, 2007). Students struggle when they don't know the vocabulary (Fisher & Frey, 2008).	In what ways do you weave the teaching of vocabulary throughout your math workshop? How do you scaffold the use of vocabulary and mathematical phraseology in the workstations?
Anecdotal records: Valuable tools for assessing young children's development. Available from: www.researchgate.net/publication/31645039_Anecdotal_records_Valuable_tools_for_assessing_young_children's_development [accessed Sep 08 2018].	Anecdotals	"Although anecdotal records can be time consuming to record and refer to, the advantages are that they provide naturalistic, detailed, and meaningful information about children's individual development in all domains" (Puckett & Black, 1993).—cited in McFarland, L. (2017). "Anecdotal Records: Valuable Tools for Assessing Children's Development." *Dimensions of Early Childhood*, 36(1), 31–36. For different examples of anecdotals also see: www.pinterest.com/drnicki7/anecdotals-in-math-workshop/	Do you have a system for keeping anecdotals? Do you set aside time to take anecdotals when students are in workstations?
Newton, N. & Nuzzie, J. (2018). *Mathematizing Your School*. New York: Routledge.	Parent involvement is crucial.	There are so many ways to get parents involved: handbooks, videos, workshops and trainings, to name a few.	Do you have a system where the parents/guardians are involved in reinforcing the priority standards at home?

Key Points

- Recording Sheets
- Self-Tracking Sheets and Self-Correcting
- Accountability to the Language
- Anecdotals
- Keeping Track of It All
- Parent Communication

Summary

It is important to know what students are doing on a day-to-day basis in the workstations (see Figure 3.5). Recording sheets help to track that information. The teacher also has to physically go and watch what is happening some days. The teacher needs to keep anecdotals on what is happening. The teacher needs to analyze the data at various levels, from a global grade level perspective, to a class perspective, to a small group of students, to the individual student (see Figure 3.9). Parents have to know how to help their students and schools have to provide that type of support to them.

Reflection Questions

1. Do you currently have a system for students to record their workstation work? How much information does it give you? How might you tweak it?
2. How often do you take anecdotals? How often do you do quick mini-interviews with your students?
3. In what ways are you in communication with parents/guardians about the individual work that their students are doing?

References

Anghileri, J. (2006). Scaffolding Practices That Enhance Mathematics Learning. *Journals of Mathematics Teacher Education*, 9(1), 33–52.

Kamii, C. & Lewis, B. A. (1990). Research into Practice: Constructivsim and First Grade-Arithmetic. *Arithmetic Teacher*, 38(1), 36–37.

Kingsdorf, S., Krawec, J., & Gritter, K. (2016). A Broad Look at the Literature on Math Word Problem-Solving Interventions for Third Graders. *Cogent Education*, 3(1). Retrieved on June 15, 2018 from https://www.cogentoa.com/article/10.1080/2331186X.2015.1135770

4

Counting Workstations

Competent counting requires mastery of a symbolic system, facility with a complicated set of procedures that require pointing at objects and designating them with symbols, and understanding that some aspects of counting are merely conventional, while others lie at the heart of its mathematical usefulness.

(Kilpatrick, Swafford, & Findell, 2001, p. 159)

Levels of Counting

Counting is a complex endeavor (see Figures 4.1 and 4.2). There are so many moving parts of the counting trajectory. The levels are nuanced, each piece adding a clearer picture to the puzzle of number sense. We need our students to know a lot of different things when it comes to counting. I am amazed every time I delve deeper into the idea of teaching counting. I think how much better we could serve

Figure 4.1 Counting

Big Ideas	Enduring Understandings
There are 20 levels of counting (Clements & Sarama, 2009). Most state standards require that kindergarteners know through level 17 (except some don't require skip counting, level 15). That is a lot of levels. Levels 18 and 19 can actually be part of other workstations. I have included level 18 as part of the early fraction workstation (during the unit of study). I have included level 19, which deals with counting to 200 and beyond, with the place value workstations. These research-based levels are very informative in terms of thinking about how we organize counting stations.	• Number words and sequence • One-to-one correspondence • Cardinality • Counting strategies and situations **Essential Questions** What does it mean to count? What are the levels of counting? Why should we level counting stations?

Figure 4.2 Counting Principles

Know/Do	
How to Count Principles (Gelman & Gallistel, 1978)	**What to Count Principles (Gelman & Gallistel, 1978)**
One-to-one The idea that there is only one distinct counting word for each item counted. **Stable Order Principle** The idea that to be able to count also means knowing that the list of words used must be in a repeatable order. **Cardinal Principle** The idea that the last word you say is the total amount.	**Abstract Principle** The idea that you can count physical and non-physical things (sounds, counting on etc.). **Order Irrelevance** The idea that it doesn't matter which order you count in as long as you count every item only once.

our students if we had the knowledge base and the language to describe what we want them to do and then the data tracking devices to see where they are along the journey.

As I discuss counting workstations, I want us to look more closely at what the levels are and how they directly shape the learning experiences that students should have at each level. For instance, at one level students might only be counting out a given set whereas in another they might be producing a set. This is so different from what usually goes on in a kindergarten classroom where they have counting jars but everyone is working on the same set of counting jars. Sometimes, there is an attempt to differentiate by having different amounts to count, which is very important but not complete. There are 20 levels of counting! That still blows my mind. I'm not suggesting that we memorize all of them, but I do believe we need to learn them, study them and have them handy when we are planning so that we can set up rich, purposeful, engaging experiences for our students.

Leveling the Stations

Station A: Correlate to Level 6

Level 6: Students should be able to count verbally to ten and have cardinality within five. They can count objects that are in a line. These are some activities for working in this workstation. In this station they are counting objects that are already out. They are not necessarily producing a count (see Figure 4.3).

Figure 4.3 Examples of Level 6

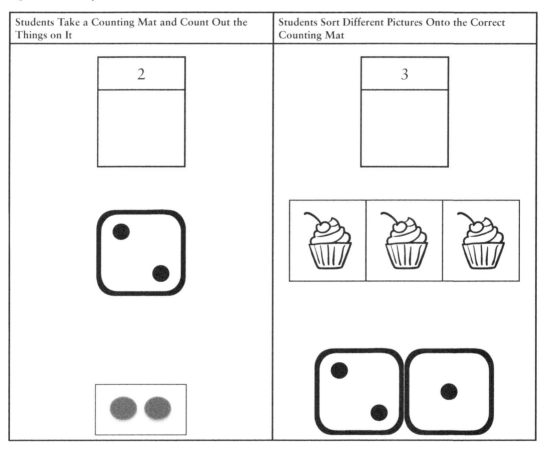

| Students Take a Counting Mat and Count Out the Things on It | Students Sort Different Pictures Onto the Correct Counting Mat |

In this level, students are not only counting objects up to 5; they are producing a count of objects at least to 4 (see Figure 4.4).

Figure 4.4 Examples of Level 7

Scaffolded Count	Producing a Count Scaffolded	Producing a Count Unscaffolded
Here, students are just counting the amount. The pictures are already there. 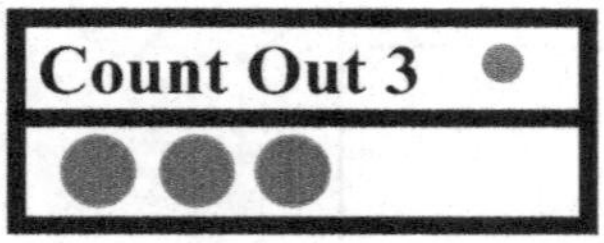	Here, the students have to produce the count. The dot lets the students know how many to count out. 	Here, the students have to produce the count but there is no scaffold. However, on the back you can have the number of dots for how many bears there should be so that students can check their work. 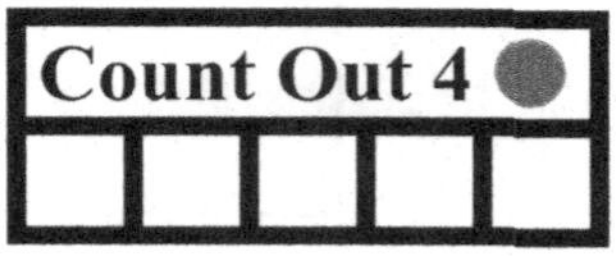 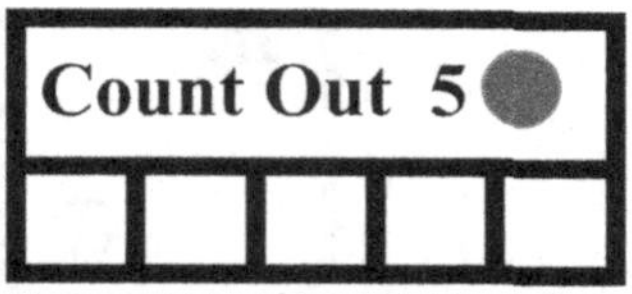
Count Out 3 ● ● ● ●	**Count Out 4** ● ▫ ▫ ▫ ▫ ▫	**Count Out 4** ● ▫ ▫ ▫ ▫ **Count Out 5** ● ▫ ▫ ▫ ▫
I can count rocket ships! 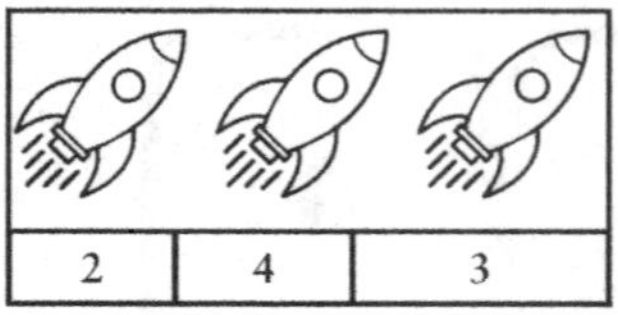 🚀 🚀 🚀 2 | 4 | 3	Count out 5 counters. 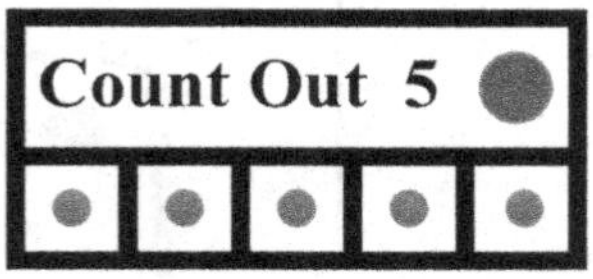 **Count Out 5** ● ▫ ▫ ▫ ▫ ▫	Count out 3 rocket ships!   🚀 🚀 🚀 🚀

At this level, students can count structured arrangements up to 10. They can produce objects with a scaffold. They can also write or draw to represent 10. Furthermore, students at this level can find the number just after or just before another number BUT only be counting up from 1 (see Figures 4.5 and 4.6).

Figure 4.5 Examples of Level 8

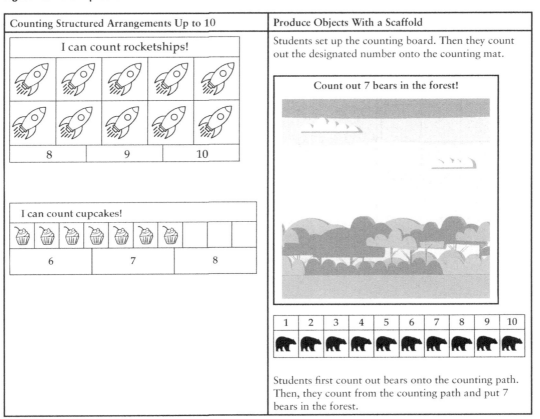

Counting Structured Arrangements Up to 10	Produce Objects With a Scaffold
I can count rocketships! (8, 9, 10) **I can count cupcakes!** (6, 7, 8)	Students set up the counting board. Then they count out the designated number onto the counting mat. **Count out 7 bears in the forest!** (1 2 3 4 5 6 7 8 9 10) Students first count out bears onto the counting path. Then, they count from the counting path and put 7 bears in the forest.

Figure 4.6 More Examples of Level 8

Write Up to 10 to Represent a Number	Draw Up to 10 to Represent a Number	Name the Number Just After or Just Before Another Number Up to 10
Trace the number that tells how many. 1 2 3 4 5 6 7 8 9 10	Draw 7 squares. Draw 6 circles.	What number comes before 8? 1, 2, 3, 4, 5, 6, ____, 8 What number comes after 8? 1, 2, 3, 4, 5, 6, 7, 8, ____ The above cards are scaffolded; these ones below are unscaffolded. What number comes before 8? 1, 2, 3, 4, 5, 6, ____, 8 What number comes after 8? 1, 2, 3, 4, 5, 6, 7, 8, ____

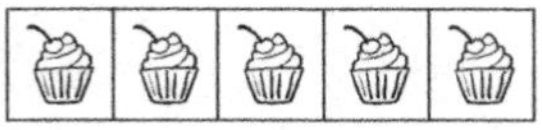

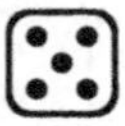

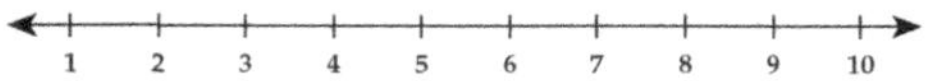

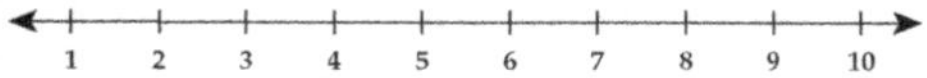

Roll it! / Write it! / Count it!

Roll it!	Write it!	Count it!
⚄	5	

Part A: Counting Objects Up to 10

Figure 4.7 Examples of Level 9

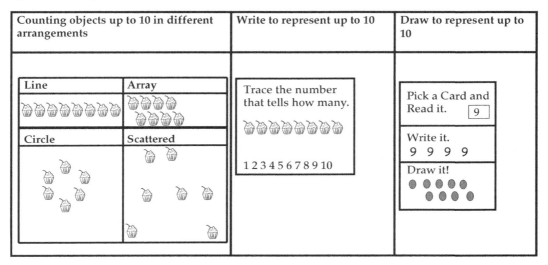

Figure 4.8 More Examples of Level 9

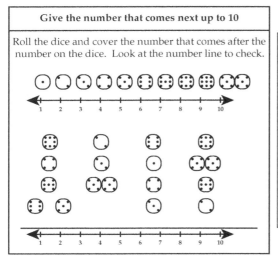

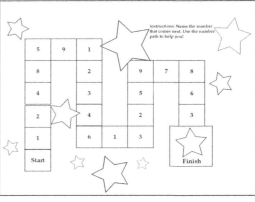

Part B: Counting Objects Up to 20 (See Figures 4.9 and 4.10)

Figure 4.9 Level 9 Ideas

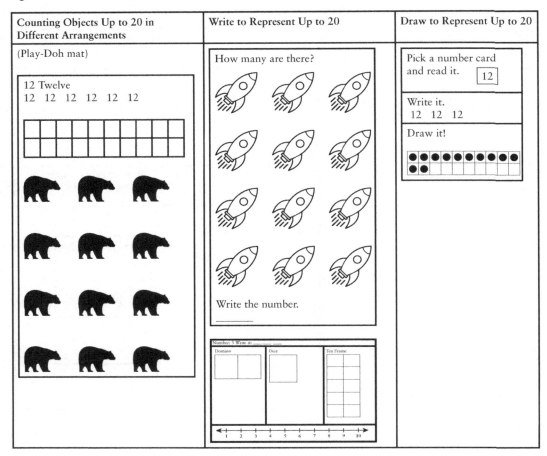

Figure 4.10 More Level 9 Ideas

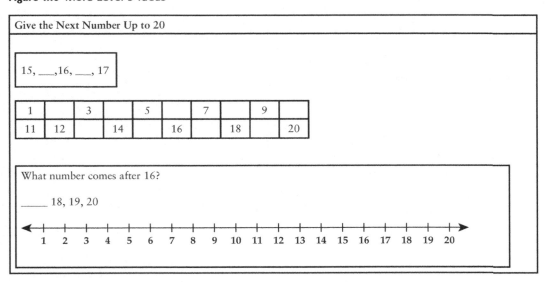

PART C: COUNTING OBJECTS UP TO 30 (SEE FIGURES 4.11–4.13)

Figure 4.11 Level 9

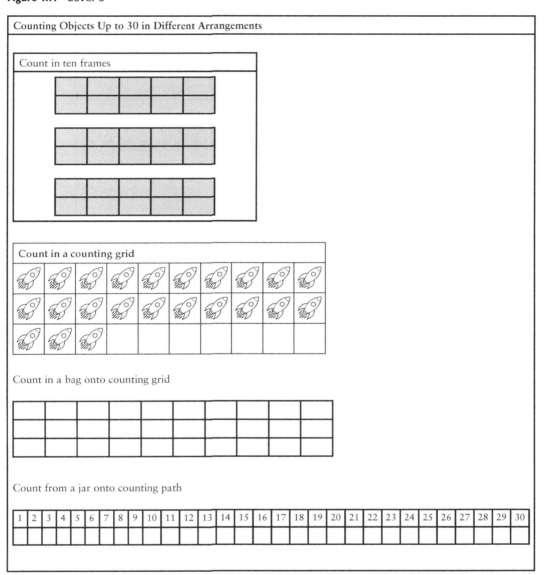

Counting Objects Up to 30 in Different Arrangements

Count in ten frames

Count in a counting grid

Count in a bag onto counting grid

Count from a jar onto counting path

1	2	3	4	5	6	7	8	9	10	11	12	13	14	15	16	17	18	19	20	21	22	23	24	25	26	27	28	29	30

Figure 4.12 Level 9

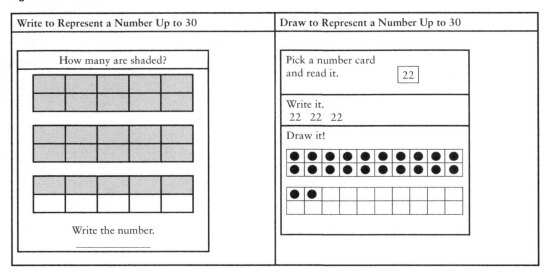

Figure 4.13 Level 9

Give the Next Number Up to 30									

25, __, 27, ___, 29

1		3	4	5	6		8		10
11		13		15		17		19	
21	22		24		26		28		30

Station E: Correlate to Level 10

At this level, students can count backwards from 10 (see Figure 4.14).

Figure 4.14 Examples of Level 10

Concrete	Pictorial	Abstract
Students use cubes to count down.	Students order the count down strips.	Students order the numbers on the blast off strip! (You can scaffold this by having one without numbers and one with numbers.)

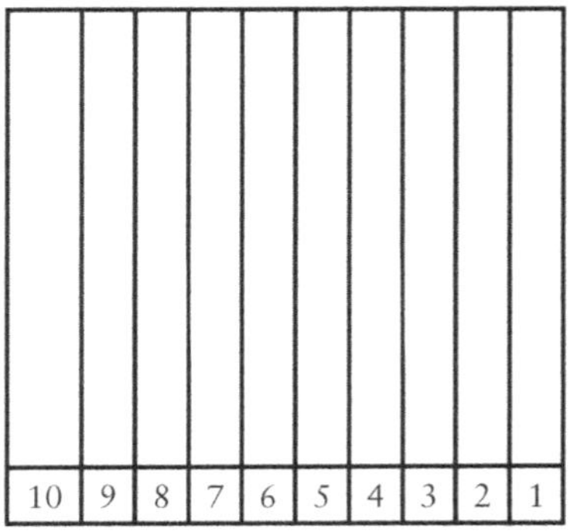

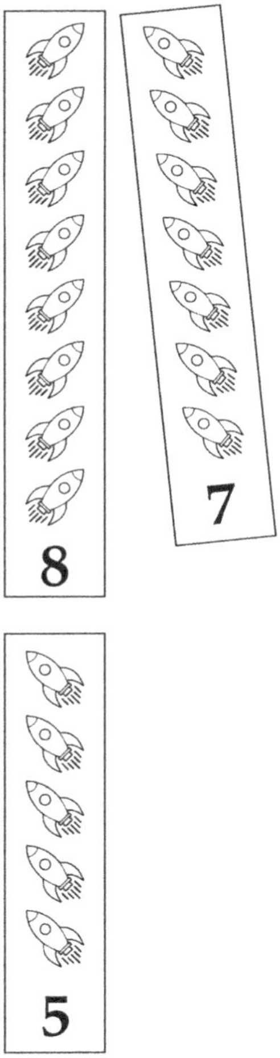

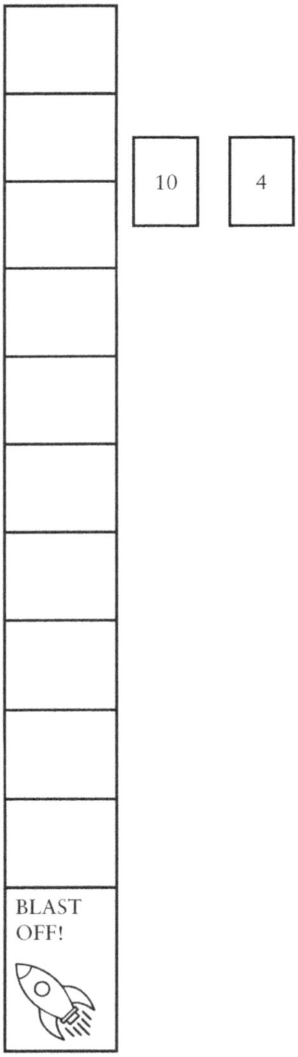

Station F: Correlates to Level 11

At this level, students start to count on, counting verbally and with objects from numbers other than 1. Children can tell you the number before and after another number without having to start at 1 (see Figure 4.15).

Figure 4.15 Examples of Level 11

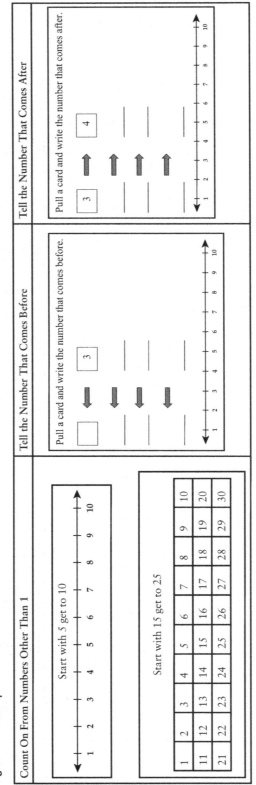

At this level, students can count by tens to 100. They can also count to 100 crossing the decades easily (see Figure 4.16).

Figure 4.16 Examples of Level 12

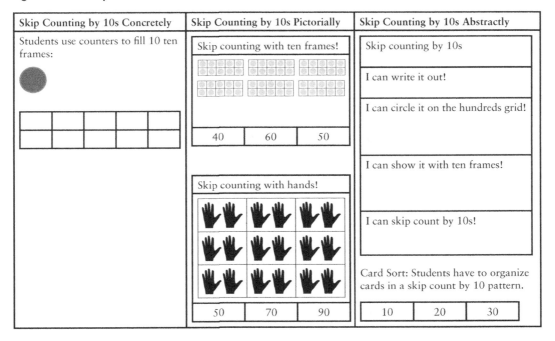

Skip Counting by 10s Concretely	Skip Counting by 10s Pictorially	Skip Counting by 10s Abstractly
Students use counters to fill 10 ten frames:	Skip counting with ten frames!	Skip counting by 10s
	40 60 50	I can write it out!
	Skip counting with hands!	I can circle it on the hundreds grid!
		I can show it with ten frames!
		I can skip count by 10s!
	50 70 90	Card Sort: Students have to organize cards in a skip count by 10 pattern.
		10 20 30

At this level, students can count by ones through 100, fluently crossing the decades, starting at any number (see Figures 4.17 and 4.18).

Figures 4.17 and **4.18** Examples of Level 13

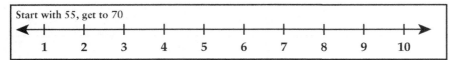

Start with 55, get to 70

| 1 | 2 | 3 | 4 | 5 | 6 | 7 | 8 | 9 | 10 |

Start with 70, get to 82

1	2	3	4	5	6	7	8	9	10
11	12	13	14	15	16	17	18	19	20
21	22	23	24	25	26	27	28	29	30
31	32	33	34	35	36	37	38	39	40
41	42	43	44	45	46	47	48	49	50
51	52	53	54	55	56	57	58	59	60
61	62	63	64	65	66	67	68	69	70
71	72	73	74	75	76	77	78	79	80
81	82	83	84	85	86	87	88	89	90
91	92	93	94	95	96	97	98	99	100

Station I: Correlate to Level 14

At this level, students can keep track of counting by using numerical patterns such as tapping (see Figure 4.19).

Figure 4.19 Examples of Level 14

Count by Finger Snapping	Count by Clapping	Count by Toe Tapping
Count from 5 to 15 with finger snaps 	Count by 2s to 12 	Count by 10s to 50 with toe taps 

At this level, students can skip count by 2s and 5s fluently (see Figures 4.20 and 4.21).

Figure 4.20 Examples of Level 15

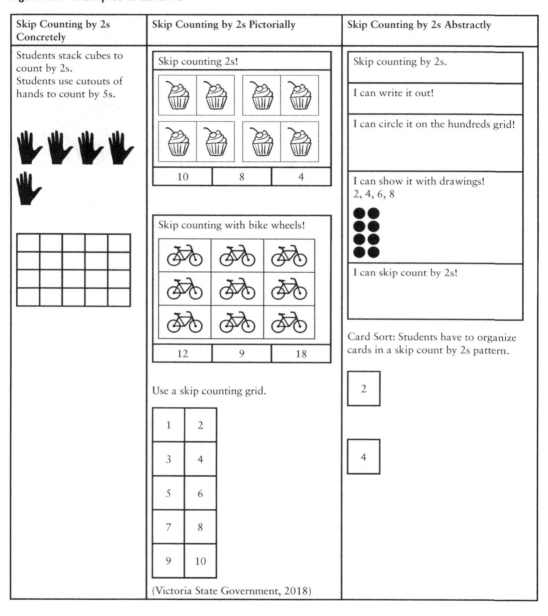

Skip Counting by 2s Concretely	Skip Counting by 2s Pictorially	Skip Counting by 2s Abstractly
Students stack cubes to count by 2s. Students use cutouts of hands to count by 5s.	Skip counting 2s! ... 10 8 4 Skip counting with bike wheels! ... 12 9 18 Use a skip counting grid. 1 2 3 4 5 6 7 8 9 10 (Victoria State Government, 2018)	Skip counting by 2s. I can write it out! I can circle it on the hundreds grid! I can show it with drawings! 2, 4, 6, 8 I can skip count by 2s! Card Sort: Students have to organize cards in a skip count by 2s pattern. 2 4

Figure 4.21 More Examples of Level 15

Skip Counting by 5s Concretely	Skip Counting by 5s Pictorially	Skip Counting by 5s Abstractly
Students use counters to fill five frames.	**Skip counting with five frames!**	Skip counting by 5s.
		I can write it out!
		I can circle it on the hundreds grid!
Students use cutouts of hands to count by 5s.		
		I can show it with five frames!
	10 | 30 | 20	
	Clip card	I can skip count by 5s!
	Skip counting the hands by 5s!	
		Card Sort: Students have to organize cards in a skip count by 5.
		10 15 5
	55 | 45 | 35	
		Use a counting grid. In this case it would be counting by 5s.

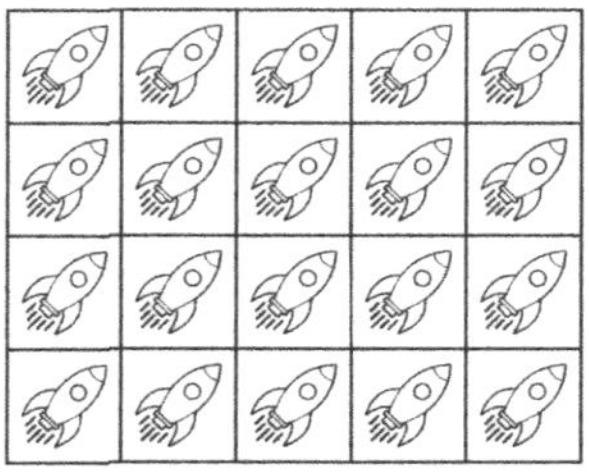

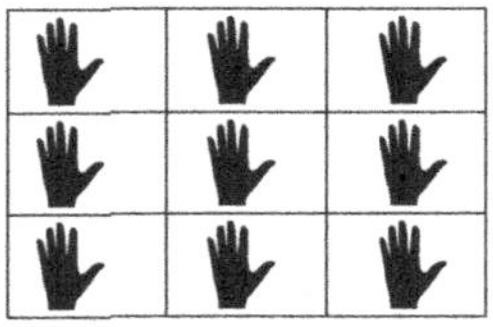

1	2	3	4	5
6	7	8	9	10
11	12	13	14	15
16	17	18	19	20
21	22	23	24	25

(Victoria State Government, 2018)

At this level, students can count mental images of hidden objects (see Figure 4.22).

Figure 4.22 Examples of Level 16

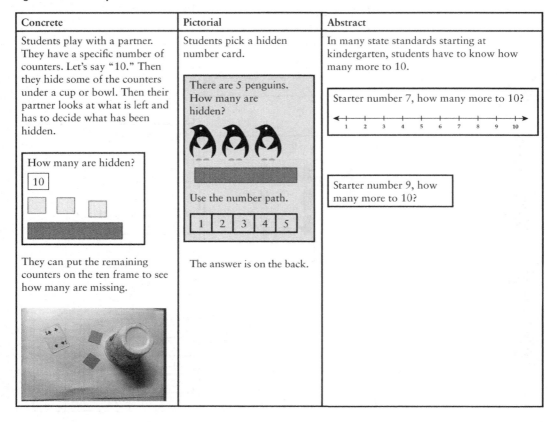

Concrete	Pictorial	Abstract
Students play with a partner. They have a specific number of counters. Let's say "10." Then they hide some of the counters under a cup or bowl. Then their partner looks at what is left and has to decide what has been hidden.	Students pick a hidden number card.	In many state standards starting at kindergarten, students have to know how many more to 10.

Concrete column:

How many are hidden?

10

They can put the remaining counters on the ten frame to see how many are missing.

Pictorial column:

There are 5 penguins. How many are hidden?

Use the number path.

| 1 | 2 | 3 | 4 | 5 |

The answer is on the back.

Abstract column:

Starter number 7, how many more to 10?

1 2 3 4 5 6 7 8 9 10

Starter number 9, how many more to 10?

Station L: Correlate to Level 17

At this level, students can count up to 4 numbers from a given number (see Figure 4.23).

Figure 4.23 Examples of Level 15

Use a Number Path

1	2	3	4	5	6	7	8	9	10
11	12	13	14	15	16	17	18	19	20

Start at 4, count up 3 more

Use a Number Grid

1	2	3	4	5	6	7	8	9	10
11	12	13	14	15	16	17	18	19	20
21	22	23	24	25	26	27	28	29	30
31	32	33	34	35	36	37	38	39	40
41	42	43	44	45	46	47	48	49	50
51	52	53	54	55	56	57	58	59	60
61	62	63	64	65	66	67	68	69	70
71	72	73	74	75	76	77	78	79	80
81	82	83	84	85	86	87	88	89	90
91	92	93	94	95	96	97	98	99	100

Start at 44, count up 4 more

Activity Card

Start at 98, count up 4 more

These last few stations are not really part of the counting station. They are part of other units, such as fractions and place value.

Station M: Correlates to Level 18

At this level students can count "unusual units such as "wholes" when shown combinations of wholes and parts. For example, they can count three whole plastic eggs and then four halves as five whole eggs." (**This would be taught with the fraction unit.**)

Station N: Correlates to Level 19

At this level students can count to 200 and beyond, recognizing place value patterns of ones, tens and hundreds. (**This station is addressed in the place value chapter.**)

Station 0: Correlates to Level 20

At this level, students can conserve a number. They understand that the number of objects does not change even if the objects are rearranged. Students can count items in a line, array, circle and scattered and understand that the number doesn't change, no matter what the arrangement is. Conservation is taught more in small groups. In the workstation students could practice finding sets of the same number in a line array, circle and scattered.

Counting Assessment

Figure 4.24 Counting Assessment

1. Teacher says: Count to 10.

Child can count to _____ correctly.
Child can count to _____ with some errors.
Notes:

---

2. Teacher says: Count these bears.

How many are there?

Child counts correctly. _____
Child counts incorrectly. _____
Notes:

5   7   10   15   20

---

3. Teacher gives the child a pile of bears and says: Count out 4 bears.

Child counts correctly. _____
Child counts incorrectly. _____
Notes:

4   7   10   14   20

4A. Teacher says: Count these rocket ships.

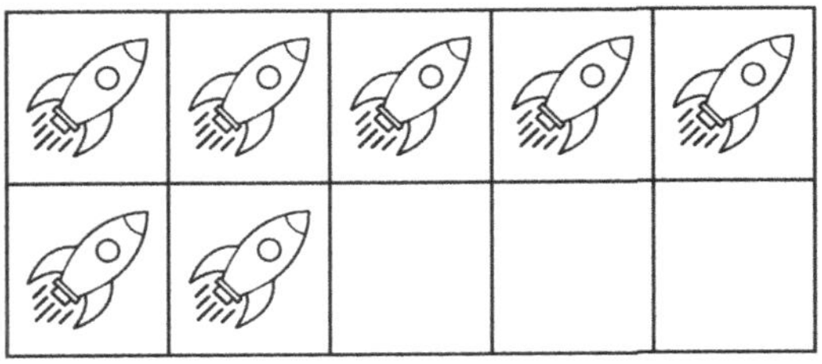

Child counts correctly. _____
Child counts incorrectly. _____
Notes:

(Continued)

Figure 4.24 Continued

Can the child count 10 items if given the items?

    B. Teacher says: Count these rocket ships.

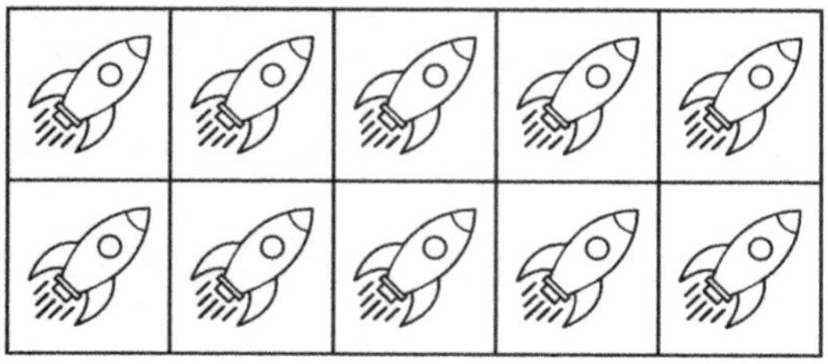

Child counts correctly. _____
Child counts incorrectly. _____
Notes:

5A. Teacher says: Draw 7 circles.

Child can draw to represent a number correctly. _____
Child draws an incorrect amount to represent a number incorrectly. _____
Notes:

5B. The teacher says: Draw 10 circles.

---

6.   The teacher says count the cupcakes in the boxes below.

A. Circle	B. Scattered

Child counts correctly. _____
Child counts incorrectly. _____
Notes:

7A. Teacher says count the rocket ships below.

B. How many are there?

Child counts correctly. _____
Child counts incorrectly. _____
Notes:

C. Teacher says: Write the number._____

Child writes number correctly. _____
Child writes number incorrectly. _____
Notes:

8. Teacher says:
    A. Write the number one: _____
    B. Write the number five: _____
    C. Write the number seven: _____
    D. Write the number nine: _____
    E. Write the number ten _____

Child writes number correctly. _____
Child writes number incorrectly. _____
Notes:

9. Teacher says: Count Backwards from 10.

Child counts correctly. _____
Child counts incorrectly. _____
Notes:

10. Teacher says:
    A. Count on from 10 to 15.
    B. Count from 12 to 20
    C. Count from 59 to 70
    D. Count from 81 to 93

Child counts correctly. _____
Child counts incorrectly. _____
Notes:

(Continued)

Figure 4.24 Continued

11. Teacher asks:
    A. What number comes before 15?
    B. What number comes before 10?
    C. What number comes before 5?

Child knows how to state the number that comes before another number correctly. _____
Child does not know how to state the number that comes before another number. _____
Notes:

12. Teacher asks: What number comes after 8?
    A. What number comes after 17?
    B. What number comes after 10?
    C. What number comes after 8?

Child knows how to state the number that comes after another number correctly. _____
Child does not know how to state the number that comes after another number. _____
Notes:

13. Teachers says: Count by 10s to 100.

Child counts correctly. _____
Child counts incorrectly. _____
Notes:

14. Teacher asks the child to count to 100 by ones.

Child counts correctly up to _____
Child counts incorrectly. _____
Notes:

15. Teacher claps and asks the child how many claps they heard.
    A. Teacher claps four times. Child answers: correct or incorrect.
    B. Teacher claps seven times. Child answers: correct or incorrect.
    C. Teacher claps ten times. Child answers: correct or incorrect.

16. Teacher asks the child how many are hidden?

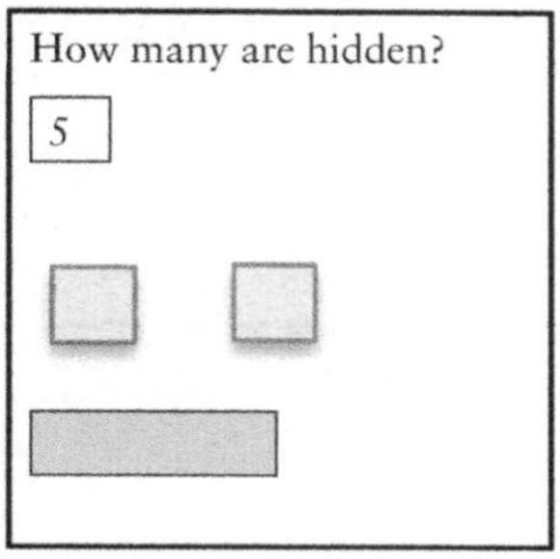

How many are hidden?

5

General Observations:

Special Notes:

Goal Setting/Helping Parents and Guardians to Help Their Children

This is a great chart to keep parents/guardians and children informed of where they are in terms of counting (see Figure 4.25).

Figure 4.25 Goal: My Counting Goals

Math	It Looks Like:	Practicing	I Know It!
Count to 10	1, 2, 3, 4, 5, 6, 7, 8, 9, 10		
Count 5 things	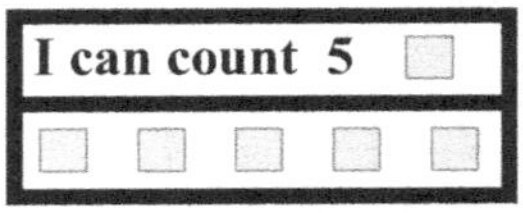 I can count 5 ☐ / ☐ ☐ ☐ ☐ ☐		
Count 10 things	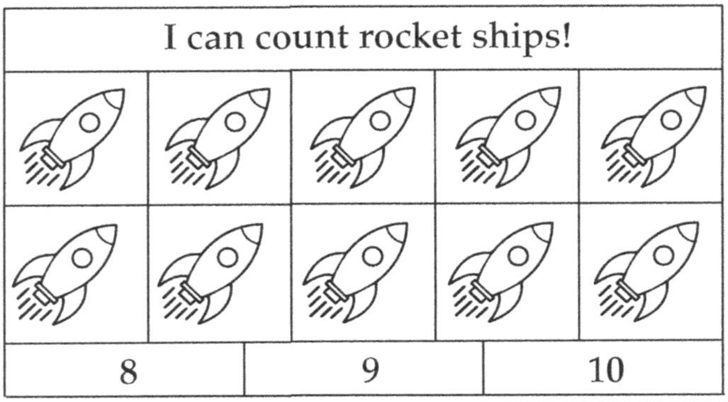 I can count rocket ships! 8 9 10		
Count backwards	10, 9, 8 . . . 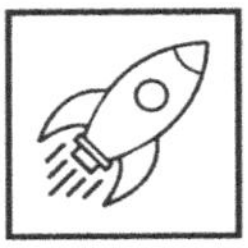		
Can count on	Start with 15, get to 25		
Count by 10s up to 100	10, 20, 30, 40, 50, 60, 70, 80, 90, 100!		

(Continued)

Figure 4.25 Continued

Math	It Looks Like:	Practicing	I Know It!
Count to 100	Start with 70, get to 82 	1	2	3	4	5	6	7	8	9	10
11	12	13	14	15	16	17	18	19	20
21	22	23	24	25	26	27	28	29	30
31	32	33	34	35	36	37	38	39	40
41	42	43	44	45	46	47	48	49	50
51	52	53	54	55	56	57	58	59	60
61	62	63	64	65	66	67	68	69	70
71	72	73	74	75	76	77	78	79	80
81	82	83	84	85	86	87	88	89	90
91	92	93	94	95	96	97	98	99	100			
Count with sounds			
Skip count by 2s and 5s	Skip counting 2s! 10 8 4		
Can count hidden numbers	How many are hidden? 10		
Can count up 3 or 4 more		1	2	3	4	5	6	7	8	9	10
11	12	13	14	15	16	17	18	19	20	 Start at 4, count up 3 more		

Figure 4.26 Class Snapshot

	Levels 1–5	L6	L7	L8	L9	L10	L11	L12	L13	L14	L15	L16	L17
Luke		x											
Tom			x										
Maritza				x									
Kelly			x										
Susie				x									
Joe			x										
Mary					x								
Kiyana					x								
Shakhira					x								
Marcus		x											
Greg	x												
Zeke	x												

Figure 4.27 Getting Started

Getting Started!

1. Make sure that you have counting boxes, bags and jars that address the different levels from the beginning. Start with doing only two or three levels.
2. Make sure to include counting in your morning routine. You could even have a count or countess that is in charge of counting something from the counting jar.
3. Be sure to have both scaffolded and unscaffolded activities from the beginning.

Researcher	Research	Big Ideas	How Does This Research Inform Our Practice?
Linda M. Platas retrieved on September 9, 2018 https://dreme.stanford.edu/news/why-and-what-counting	Play should be an important part of the teaching and learning of math concepts and skills.	"Math should be intentional, purposeful and playful." In early childhood settings. There should be times for both "Planned and Spontaneous counting opportunities."	Do you have playful, intentional and purposeful activities in your counting workstations?
Reed, K. & Young, J. retrieved on Sept. 9, 2018 from https://dreme.stanford.edu/news/math-games-excite-young-minds	Math games should not only be used to teach math but also socio-emotional skills.	"Math games give structure and process, develop independence and perseverance and foster social-emotional development like being patient, taking turns, and solving problems collaboratively. [They] also [can develop] a sense of competition-winning and losing with dignity."	Do you use intentional games in your math workstations? How do you teach and reinforce the social skills that students need to successfully participate in games?
Wellman, H. & Miller, K. (1986). Thinking About Nothing: Development of Concepts of Zero. *British Journal of Developmental Psychology*, 4(1), 31–42. Retrieved on September 15, 2018 from https://onlinelibrary.wiley.com/doi/abs/10.1111/j.2044-835X.1986.tb00995.x Merrit, D. & Brannon, E. (2013). Nothing to it: Precursors to a Zero Concept in Preschoolers. *Behavioural Processes*, 93, 91–97. Retrieved on Oct. 5, 2018 from https://www.ncbi.nlm.nih.gov/pmc/articles/PMC3582820	It takes more than a day to teach and learn about the number 0.	Many researchers have found that zero is a difficult concept to understand. We count from 1 so zero isn't part of the counting numbers. The idea of zero meaning no quantity is hard for students to understand. Students need many experiences with this concept to fully grasp it.	Do you assess students for their understanding of zero? What types of games and activities do you do in workstations so that students can work with this concept across the year?
Clements, D. H. & Sarama, J. (2014). The Importance of the Early Years. In R. E. Slavin (Ed.), *Science, Technology & Mathematics (STEM)*, pp. 5–9. Thousand Oaks, CA: Corwin. Cross, C., Woods, T. & Schweingruber, H. (Eds.) (2009). *Mathematics Learning in Early Childhood: Paths Towards Excellence in Equity*. Washington, DC: Committee on Early Childhood Mathematics; National Research Council. Fosnot, C. T. & Dolk, M. (2001). *Young Mathematicians at Work: Constructing Number Sense, Addition, and Substraction*. Portsmouth, NH: Heinemann. Fuson, K.C. (2012). The Common Core Mathematics Standards as Supports for Learning and Teaching Early and Elementary School. In J.S. Carlson & J.R. Levine (Eds.) *Instructional Strategies for Improving Student Learning: Focus on Early Mathematics and Reading*, Psychological Perspectives on Contemporary Educational Issues Vol. 3, pp. 177–186. Charlotte, NC: Information Age Publishing.	Counting is a very complex endeavor. There are many factors involved.	Teachers have to be aware of the many different types of errors that students make so they can scaffold learning to count.	What is the practice, demonstration and scaffolding that you do throughout the year to develop counting skills? How do you scaffold progressively more challenging counting activities throughout the year?

Researcher	Research	Big Ideas	How Does This Research Inform Our Practice?
Siegler, R. S. & Ramani, G. B. (2009). Playing Linear Number Board Games—But Not Circular Ones—Improves Low-Income Preschoolers' Numerical Understanding. *Journal of Educational Psychology*, 101(3), 545–560.	Games are an excellent way to teach many different number sense activities in the primary grades.	They found significant differences in developing number sense between linear and circular board games. We should use linear ones. They also found that spacing, numbers and an obvious start and finish mattered.	Do you currently use linear games in your workstations to develop number sequence, magnitude and number line estimation?

Class Snapshot

Key Points

- Several Levels
- Concrete, Pictorial, Abstract
- Scaffolded and Unscaffolded Activities

Summary

There are 20 levels of counting. Most workstation activities start at about level 6. There are some significant nuanced differences between the levels. Knowing these differences and planning activities so that students can work at the appropriate level is what makes all the difference between students being frustrated and bored or learning. We all have to commit to getting better at knowing the levels of counting so that we can give our primary students a firm foundation for the concepts they will encounter in the later grades. It is important to have good assessments and ways for parents and students to know how they are progressing (see Figures 4.26–4.28).

Reflection Questions

1. How do you currently frame your teaching and learning environments around the counting levels?
2. What have you learned in this chapter?
3. What will you do with the information?

References

Clements, D. H. & Sarama, J. (2014). *Learning and Teaching Early Math: The Learning Trajectories Approach (2nd ed.)*: New York, NY: Routledge.

Cross, C. T., Woods, T. A., & Schweingruber, H. (2009). *Mathematics Learning in Early Childhood*. Washington, DC: National Academies Press.

Fosnot, C. & Dolk, M. (2001). *Young Mathematicians at Work: Constructing Number Sense, Addition and Subtraction*. Portsmouth, NH: Heinemann.

Fuson, K. C. (2012). *Children's Counting and Concepts of Number*. New York, NY: Springer-Verlag

Gelman, R. & Gallistel, C. (1978). *The Child's Understanding of Number*. Cambridge, MA: Harvard University Press.

Kilpatrick, J., Swafford, J. & Findell, B. (2001). *Adding It Up: Helping Children Learn Mathematics*. Washington, DC: National Academy of Sciences—National Research Council. www.nap.edu/catalog/9822.html.

Victoria State Government. (2018). www.education.vic.gov.au/school/teachers/teachingresources/discipline/maths/continuum/Pages/advskipcount25.aspx.

Wellman, H. M., & Miller, K. F. (1986). Thinking About Nothing: Development of Concepts of Zero. *British Journal of Developmental Psychology*, 4(1), 31–42.

5

Number Workstations

Number is a complex and multifaceted concept. A well-developed understanding of number includes a grasp not only of counting and numeral recognition but also of a complex system of more-and-less relationships, part-whole relationships, the role of special numbers such as five and ten, connections between numbers and real quantities and measures in the environment, and much more.

(Ontario Ministry of Education and Training, 1997, p. 10)

Part A: Exploring Number

There are so many different things that we want students to know about numbers (see Figure 5.1). There are different levels when exploring them. In this chapter we are going to look at two important aspects of exploring numbers, subitizing and composing and decomposing. There are actually ten levels of subitizing and five levels of composing and decomposing (Clements & Sarama, 2009). In terms of workstations in the primary grades we are concerned with levels 5 to 9 for subitizing. We are only concerned with levels 3 to 5 for composing and decomposing.

Figure 5.1 Counting

Big Ideas Each number can be represented differently, and in many ways. Subitizing is "instantly seeing how many" (Clements, 1999, p. 402) "automatically without having to engage in conscious counting" (Wynn, 1995, p. 36).	
Perceptual	Conceptual
"recognizing a number without using other mathematical processes, for example children might 'see 3' without any learned mathematical knowledge" (Clements, 1999, p. 2).	"more advanced ability to group and quantify sets quickly that in turn supports their development of number sense and arithmetic abilities" (Clements, 1999, p. 2). Subitizing is a foundation skill for counting forward and backwards, for counting on and in groups, adding, subtracting and later on multiplication (Steffe & Cobb, 1988; Reys et al., 2012).
Enduring Understandings • Numbers can be represented in many different ways • We can put together numbers • We can take apart numbers	
Essential Questions Why is it important for students to know how to subitize? How do we scaffold the subitizing and composing and decomposing workstations to meet the needs of individual learners?	Know/Do Subitize both perceptually and conceptually. Compose numbers. Decompose numbers.

Part B: Subitizing

I have seen some really great subitizing workstations. One of the best ones that I've ever seen was in a kindergarten class. There were 3 students. One of the students was the "teacher." That student would flash a ten frame with different numbers of dots to the other two students. Then those two students had a ten frame in front of them and they would try to set it up to match what they saw. Whoever did it first won. But it didn't really matter; they would just laugh and keep on playing. After about five turns, they would switch "teachers." The students were on task and really practicing in a purposeful way.

Station A: Level 5

Station A: Perceptual Subitizer to 5 (see Figure 5.2)

At this level, students can instantly recognize small collections up to 5 and verbally name them. The child tells the amount. For example if they see 4 on the dice, they would say 4. They are focusing on what they see.

Figure 5.2 Activities for Perceptual Subitizing to 5

Dice: Students Roll the Dice and Name How Many Dots They See to Their Partner. You Could Also Add an Element Where They Each Take a Turn and Whoever Has the Bigger Number Wins a Point or Gets a Cube. Whoever has Ten Cubes First Wins. 	Five Frames: Students Pick Up a Five Frame and Name How Many Objects They See to Their Partner. You Could Also Add an Element Where They Each Take a Turn and Whoever Has the Bigger Number Wins a Point or Gets a Cube. Whoever Has Ten Cubes First Wins. 	Dominos: Students Pick Up a Domino and Name How Many Objects They See to Their Partner. You Could Also Add an Element Where They Each Take a Turn and Whoever Has the Bigger Number Wins a Point or Gets a Cube. Whoever Has Ten Cubes First Wins. 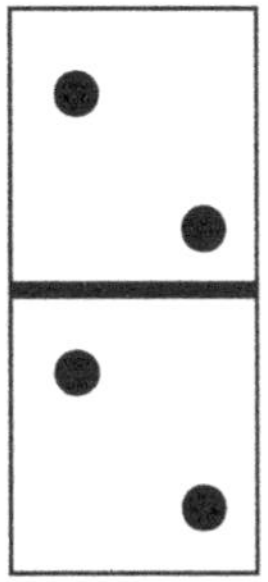

(Continued)

Figure 5.2 Continued

Card Game: Students Pull a Card and Name How Many Items They See to Their Partner. You Could Also Add an Element Where They Each Take a Turn and Whoever Has the Bigger Number Wins a Point or Gets a Cube. Whoever Has Ten Cubes First Wins.

Board Game: Students Roll the Dice and Move Around the Board That Many Spaces. When They Land on the Space They Have to Say How Many. If They Are Incorrect, They Just Have to Correct It to Stay There. Whoever Reaches Finish First Wins.

Counting Race

Instructions: Pick a card. Person with highest number starts. Players take turns picking a card and moving that many spaces. Player must count how many animals are on the space where they land. If incorrect, player stays on their space. The first person to get to finish wins.

Roll and Color Number Races: Students Roll the Dice and Shade the Number. It Is a Collaborative Game and the Students Work Together to Shade All the Numbers.

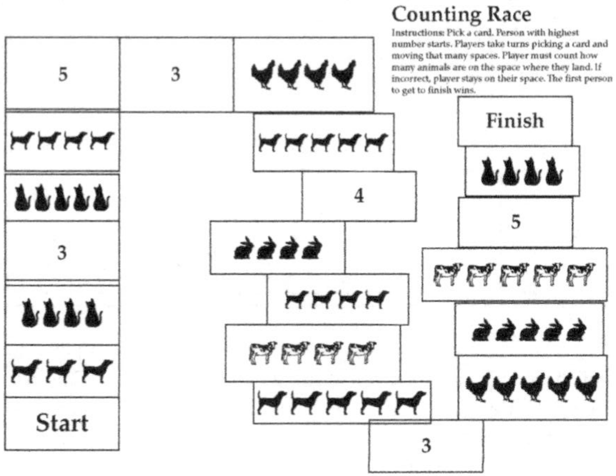

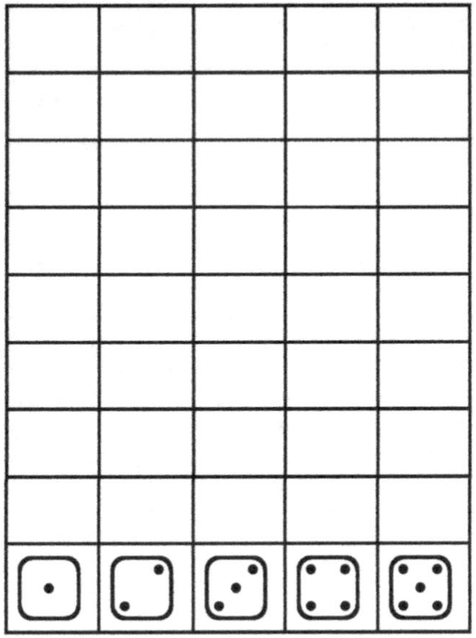

Station B: Level 6: Conceptual Subitizer to 5+ (see Figures 5.3 and 5.4)

At this level, students can instantly recognize small collections up to 5 and verbally name them. The child tells how they saw it. **They can break it down into parts and wholes.** For example if they see 4 on the dice, they might say I saw 2 and 2. They are focusing on what they see. It is important to follow some of the research suggested representations. Van de Walle (2007) suggested various dot representations and so did Kathy Richardson (2012). Clements (1999) discusses some ways to do it as well. This is really important because through the use of arrangements and color, students get the opportunity to focus on how the number can be made. **Students can also listen to, watch and sing along with the many subitizing games online.**

Figure 5.3 Activities for Conceptual Subitizing to 5+

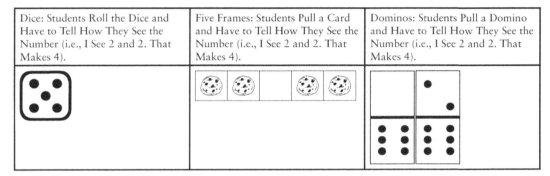

Dice: Students Roll the Dice and Have to Tell How They See the Number (i.e., I See 2 and 2. That Makes 4).	Five Frames: Students Pull a Card and Have to Tell How They See the Number (i.e., I See 2 and 2. That Makes 4).	Dominos: Students Pull a Domino and Have to Tell How They See the Number (i.e., I See 2 and 2. That Makes 4).

Figure 5.4 More Subitizing Activities

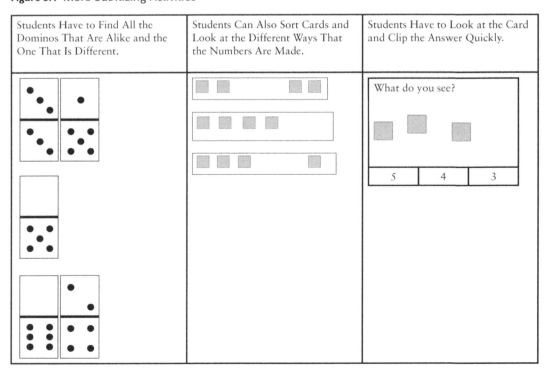

Students Have to Find All the Dominos That Are Alike and the One That Is Different.	Students Can Also Sort Cards and Look at the Different Ways That the Numbers Are Made.	Students Have to Look at the Card and Clip the Answer Quickly.

Station C: Level 7: Conceptual Subitizer to 10 (see Figures 5.5 and 5.6)

At this level, students can instantly recognize arrangements up to 10 and verbally name them. This should be scaffolded with concentrated work on each number and the different ways to see that number. The child tells the way that they saw it. For example if they see 8 on the dice, they might say I saw 4 and 4. They are focusing on what they see.

Figure 5.5 Activities for Subitizing to 10

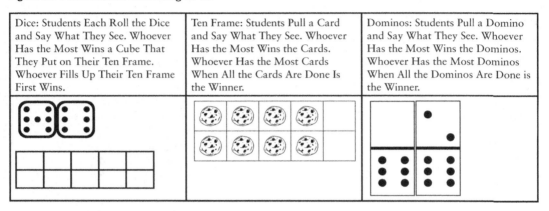

| Dice: Students Each Roll the Dice and Say What They See. Whoever Has the Most Wins a Cube That They Put on Their Ten Frame. Whoever Fills Up Their Ten Frame First Wins. | Ten Frame: Students Pull a Card and Say What They See. Whoever Has the Most Wins the Cards. Whoever Has the Most Cards When All the Cards Are Done Is the Winner. | Dominos: Students Pull a Domino and Say What They See. Whoever Has the Most Wins the Dominos. Whoever Has the Most Dominos When All the Dominos Are Done is the Winner. |

Figure 5.6 More Activities for Subitizing to 10

| Concentration: Students Lay Out All the Cards in a 3 by 4 Array. They Then Take Turns Turning Over Two Cards Trying to Find a Match. 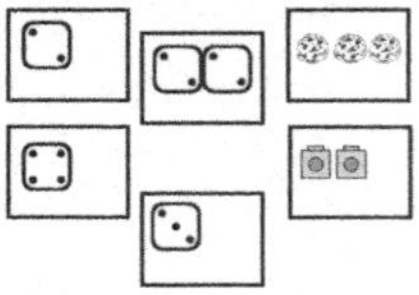 | Students Can Play a Board Game Where They Have to Subitize the Number They Land On. The First Person to Reach Finish Wins. 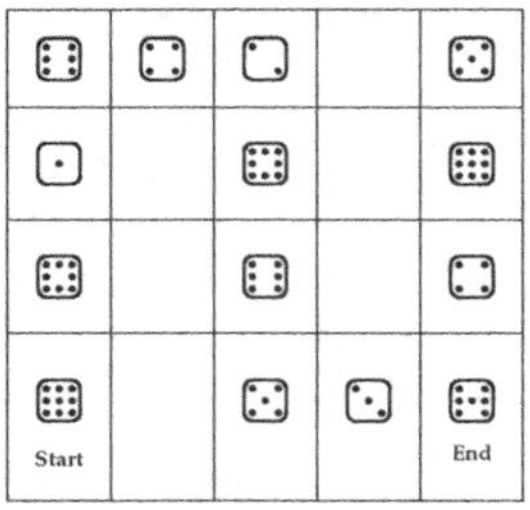 | Students Can Play Subitizing Bingo. They Pull a Card and Have to Find That Many on Their Board. Whoever Gets Four in a Row First Wins. 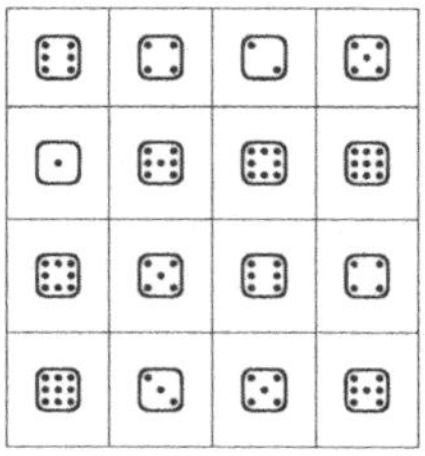 |

Station D: Level 8: Conceptual Subitizer to 20 (see Figure 5.7)

At this level, students can verbally label and discuss structured arrangements up to 20 and verbally name them. This should be scaffolded with concentrated work on each number and the different ways to see that number. The child tells the way that they saw it. For example if they see 12 they might say I saw 6 and 6. They are focusing on what they see.

Figure 5.7 Activities for Subitizing to 20

Dice	Double Ten Frame	Dominos
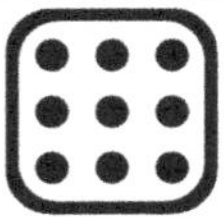	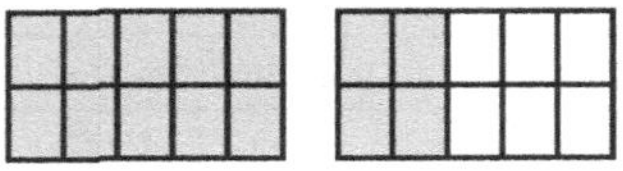	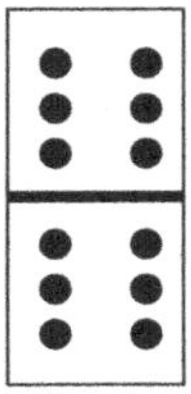

Station E: Level 9: Conceptual Subitizer With Place Value and Skip Counting (see Figure 5.8)

At this level, students are able to look at numbers and see patterns of skip counting and use their understanding of place value to verbally label structured arrangements shown quickly. The child tells the way that they saw it. For example if they see 35, they might say I saw three 10s and five 1s. It is important that we continue to subitize with the hundreds grid and the ten frames because it reinforces this place value. Students would be flashing these frames and their partners would be saying what they saw. On the back of the card it could have the answer three 10s and five 1s and that makes 35.

Figure 5.8 Activities for Level 9

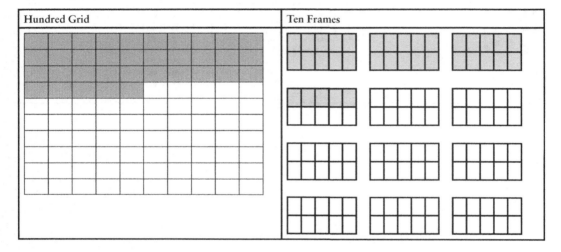

Station F: Subitizing level 10 is about using place value and looking at arrangements for multiplication and eventually decimals. This would not be in the K-2 workstations.

Part C: Composing and Decomposing

Composing and decomposing is a very important skill set that we want young children to develop well in kindergarten (see sidebar). It leads directly down the path to addition and subtraction. In kindergarten centers, students typically start at level 3 and work all the way through to level 5. However, you could have some first and even some second graders that are still struggling with composing to 10 (which is level 5). The activities at the levels are primarily the same but the number ranges vary. This is important so that students build a firm foundation working with lower numbers and adding numbers as they grow along the developmental path.

Richardson (1997) notes that "in grade 1, work with part-part-whole mats builds on students' understanding of composing and decomposing numbers."

Station A: Level 3 (Composer to 4, then 5) (see Figure 5.9)

At this level, students begin to know number combinations. The students can name the parts of a whole and the whole of the parts. Students at this level are working on putting together and taking apart 4 and then 5. There are a variety of activities that students should work with to develop this idea of composing and decomposing. In the example activity below, students are given five frames and pictures of cats and dogs. They have to figure out all the ways they can make 5 with the pictures.

Figure 5.9 Activities for Level 3

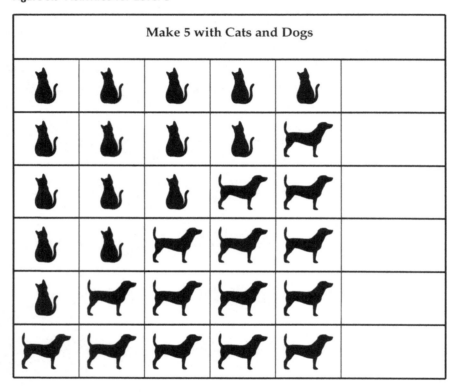

Station B: Level 4 (Composer to 7) (see Figure 5.10)

At this level, students are working on number combinations to 7. Students are getting more comfortable with putting numbers together and breaking them apart. They can also double numbers to 10. In the example below, students can do this on their iPad, laptop or a desktop. They are using the Math Learning Center app and finding ways to make 7. Now there is the traditional spill and count game with two-colored counters, which students should definitely do, but they should also get to practice this skill digitally when possible.

Figure 5.10 Activities for Level 4

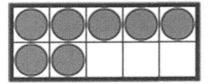 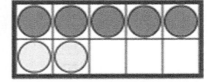

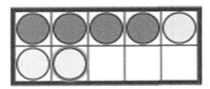

Station C: Level 5 (Composer to 10) (see Figure 5.11)

At this level, students are working on number combinations to 10. They can double numbers to 20. Combinations to 10 are really important. We have to have lots of different ways for students to explore this at the concrete, pictorial and abstract levels. Students can also listen to videos about this at the workstation. There are several animated videos about partners of 10.

Figure 5.11 Activities for Level 5

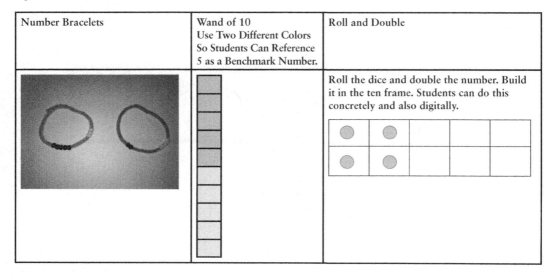

Number Bracelets	Wand of 10 Use Two Different Colors So Students Can Reference 5 as a Benchmark Number.	Roll and Double
		Roll the dice and double the number. Build it in the ten frame. Students can do this concretely and also digitally.

Keeping Students Accountable

Here are examples of recording sheets for composing and decomposing (see Figure 5.12).

Figure 5.12 Examples of Keeping Track of Progress

Recording Sheet	Recording Sheet
Pull a card. Show different ways to make it on the rekenrek. Draw it. Name: Date: Draw What You Did on the Rekenrek! _____ + _____	Throw ten counters in the pie pan and record how they landed.

Helping Parents/Guardians Help Their Children

Figure 5.13 shows an example of a letter to parents/guardians about composing and decomposing.

Figure 5.13 Parent/Guardian Letter

Dear Parents/Guardians,
We are learning how to compose (put together) and decompose (break apart) numbers. Your student is working on level 10. In this level we are working on composing and decomposing numbers to 10. Here is a rekenrek to work with at home. Please have your child show you different ways to make numbers to 10. Then, have your child explain what they did. They can do it with the hands-on rekenrek that we sent. Also, they can do it online with a virtual rekenrek: https://apps.mathlearningcenter.org/number-rack/

For example:

3 and 4 is a way to make 7.
4 and 3 is a way to make 7.
5 and 2 is a way to make 7.

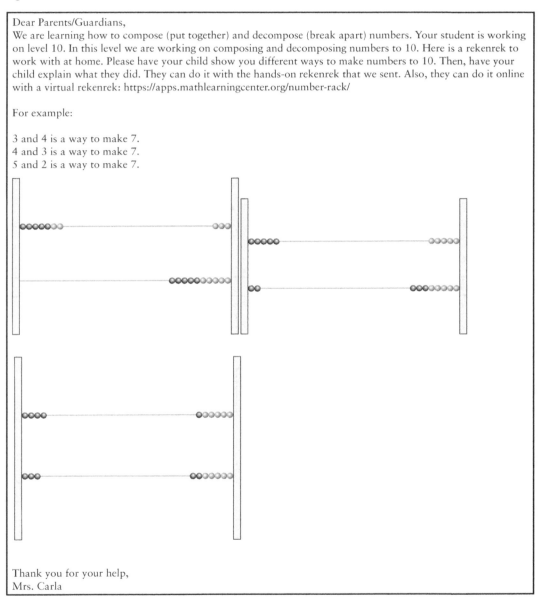

Thank you for your help,
Mrs. Carla

Keeping Track of It All

Subitizing Assessments (see Figures 5.14–5.16)

Figure 5.14 Assessing Subitizing

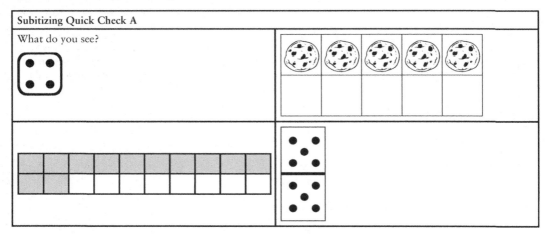

Subitizing Quick Check A

What do you see?

Figure 5.15 Assessing Subitizing

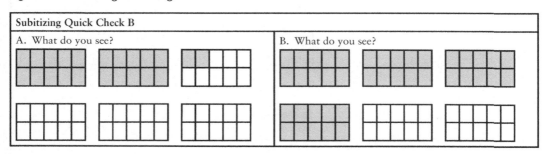

Subitizing Quick Check B

A. What do you see?

B. What do you see?

Figure 5.16 Class Snapshot

Subitizing	Level 5	Level 6	Level 7	Level 8	Level 9
Luke	x				
Tom	x				
Maritza	x				
Kelly	x				
Susie		x			
Joe		x			
Mary		x			
Kiyana		x			
Shakhira			x		
Marcus			x		
Greg			x		
Zeke			x		

Composing and Decomposing Assessment (see Figures 5.17 and 5.18)

Figure 5.17 Assessing Composing and Decomposing

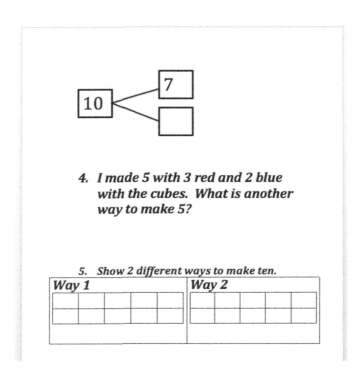

Quick Check

1. *Draw the rest of the balls to make 5.*

2 and _____ make 5.

2.
   Draw the rest of the balls to make 7.

5 and _____ make 7.

3. *Complete the number bonds*

5 — 4 / ☐

10 — 7 / ☐

4. *I made 5 with 3 red and 2 blue with the cubes. What is another way to make 5?*

5. *Show 2 different ways to make ten.*

Way 1	Way 2

Number Workstations ◆ 67

Figure 5.18 Class Snapshot

Composing and Decomposing	Level 3	Level 4	Level 5
Luke	x		
Tom	x		
Maritza	x		
Kelly	x		
Susie		x	
Joe		x	
Mary		x	
Kiyana		x	
Shakhira			x
Marcus			x
Greg			x
Zeke			x

Figure 5.19

Getting Started!

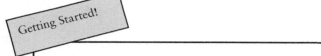

1. Make sure that you have a subitizing toolkit: dice, dominos, ten frames, dot cards and hundred grids.
2. Make sure that you set up subitizing and composing and decomposing workstations from the beginning of the year.

Researcher	Research	Big Ideas	How Does This Research Inform Our Practice?
Ma, L. (1999). *Knowing and Teaching Elementary Mathematics: Teachers' Understanding of Fundamental Mathematics in China and the United States.* Mahwah, N.J: Lawrence Erlbaum Associates.	Composing and decomposing numbers is key to addition and subtraction.	Ma looked at composing and decomposing among young children in China and other East Asian countries. She maintains that teaching children to compose and decompose numbers is the foundation to addition and subtraction.	Is there a focus on composing and decomposing numbers in your class and at your grade?
Richardson, K. (2012). *How Children Learn Number Concepts: A Guide to the Critical Learning Phases.* Bellingham, WA: Math Perspectives Teacher Development Center.	She found that we rush children too quickly to the next concept when we think they understand something. We need to work on complexifying the thinking with smaller numbers.	She notes that we sometimes rush to the next level without thinking about extending the current level into richer thinking. She argues that we should delve deep into building number sense concepts with smaller numbers before stretching to larger ones.	Think about what you do in situations where students know concepts really well. How do you further that thinking?
Baroody, A. (1987). *Children's Mathematical Thinking: A Developmental Framework for Preschool, Primary and Special Education.* New York: Teachers College Press.	Subitizing is very important and we need to put more emphasis on how it is scaffolded throughout the year.	Research shows that subitizing is a "fundamental skill in the development of students' understanding of number."	How much emphasis is put on subitizing in your class and at your grade level? What opportunities do students have to practice this throughout the year in the workstations?
Chapin, S. H. & Johnson, A. (2006). *Math Matters: Understanding the Math You Teach, Grades K–8.* Sausalito, CA: Math Solutions Publications.	We should focus on part-whole understandings rather than counting by ones.	"Research indicates that students instructed using a part-whole approach do *significantly better* with number concepts, problem solving, and place value than those students whose instruction focuses just on counting by ones."	How much of an emphasis do you put on part-whole understandings with your students in their workstations?
Van de Walle, J. A., Lovin, L., Karp, K. & Bay-Williams, J. (2018). *Teaching Student-Centered Mathematics.* New York: Pearson Education.	We have to emphasize part-whole relationships in the curriculum.	"The ability to think of a number in terms of parts is a major milestone in the development of number sense. Of the 4 different types of relationships that children can and should develop with numbers (Spatial, One and Two More, One and Two Less, Anchors or Benchmarks of 5 and 10, Part-part-whole), part-whole ideas are *easily the most important.*"	How carefully have you thought about the four different types of relationships and how they are integrated continually throughout your workstations so that students get distributed practice across the year?
Gracia-Bafalluy, M. & Noël, M.P. (2008). *Does Finger Training Increase Young Children's Numerical Performance?* Retrieved on September 10th, 2018 from www.ncbi.nlm.nih.gov/pubmed/18387567	Fingers are important.	"And studies show that young children with good finger awareness are better at performing quantitative tasks than those with less finger sense."	How well does your school emphasize and work with fingers throughout kindergarten and the beginnings of first grade? What types of finger activities do you integrate throughout the workstations, such as card games and board games that show finger representations?

Key Points

- Exploring Number
- Subitizing
- Composing and Decomposing

Summary

In the primary grades, subitizing and composing and decomposing numbers are essential ongoing activities. They both have learning trajectories that educators have to consider when designing workstation activities. Both of these skills lay the foundation for addition and subtraction. Students who are proficient in both these skills have very little trouble moving into adding and subtracting because they have been working with, seeing and playing around with numbers in numerous ways. There are so many things to do with subitizing and composing and decomposing numbers throughout the workshop; however, in this chapter I have limited the discussion to what that looks like specifically in the workstations (see Figures 5.19 and 5.20).

Reflection Questions

1. Do you have a system for knowing at what levels your students are subitizing? Do you have a teacher subitizing kit? Do you do it often?
2. Do you know at what levels your students are with composing and decomposing numbers?
3. Since composing and decomposing numbers and subitizing are such foundational concepts for adding and subtracting, how do you incorporate them throughout the year? How do you involve parents in these key activities?

References

Baroody, A. J. (1987). *Children's Mathematical Thinking: A Developmental Framework for Preschool, Primary, and Special Education Teachers*. New York, N.Y.: Teachers College Press.

Clements, D. H. (1999). *Subitizing, What Is It? Why Teach It? Teaching Children Mathematics*. Reston, VA.

Clements, D. H. & Sarama, J. (2009) *Learning and Teaching Early Math: The Learning Trajectories Approach*. New York: Routledge.

Ontario Ministry of Education and Training. (1997). *The Ontario Curriculum, Grades 1–8: Mathematics*. Toronto: Author.

Reys, R. E., Lindquist, M. M., Lambdin, D. V., Smith, N. L., Rogers, A., Falle, J., Frid, S. & Bennett, S. (2012). *Helping Children Learn Mathematics*. Australia: John Wiley & Sons, Ltd.

Richardson, K. (1997). Math Time: The Learning Environment. In Karen Antell (Ed.), *Educational Enrichment*.

Richardson, K. (2012). *How Children Learn Number Concepts: A Guide to the Critical Learning Phases*. Bellingham, WA: Math Perspectives Teacher Development Center.

Steffe, Leslie P. & Cobb, P. (1988). *Construction of Arithmetical Meanings and Strategies*. New York: Springer-Verlag.

Van de Walle, John A. (2007). *Elementary and Middle School Mathematics: Teaching Developmentally*. Boston: Pearson, Allyn and Bacon.

Wynn, K. (1995). Origins of Numerical Knowledge. *Mathematical Cognition*, 1, 35–60.

6

Place Value Workstations

Being able to procedurally do the math is necessary but not sufficient!

Place Value Is the Glue to Number Sense

Place value is so important. It's way more than a unit of study. It is a way of life. It is how we frame much of our mathematical understandings. We have to give it its rightful place in the curriculum. We have to design workstations that give deep practice all year long so that students come away with a profound sense of place and value of numbers (see sidebar).

Leveling Place Value workstations is framed around the idea that students should be solidifying the standards from the grade before as they are learning their new grade level standards (see Figure 6.1). In kindergarten, you don't really even put up the place value workstation until sometime in early spring. In first and second grade, you should start the year off with the place value workstation as part of the rotations. Students should be reviewing the place value concepts and skills from prior grades. To know where students should begin their practice, you have to give a place value assessment from the end of the last year. This is so important because students are not necessarily entering the new grade with the things they left knowing in the prior grade. After the assessment, the data is used to inform where students should be purposefully practicing.

Students should be able to "consider analogous problems, represent problems coherently, justify conclusions, apply the mathematics to practical situations, use technology mindfully to work with the mathematics, explain the mathematics accurately to other students, step back for an overview or deviate from a known procedure to find a shortcut."
(National Governors Association Center for Best Practices, 2010, p. 8)

Figure 6.1 Place Value

Big Ideas in K–2 Numbers have a place and a value. There are many ways to represent numbers. There are many different strategies to add and subtract numbers.	Enduring Understandings Understand base ten system of ones, tens and hundreds.
Essential Questions What is place value? How do we use 1s, 10s and 100s to make numbers? Why is place value important?	Know/Do Represent numbers in different ways. Skip count by 2s, 5s, and 10s. Compare numbers. Add and subtract 10 and 100 to and from numbers. Add and subtract up to three-digit numbers with three-digit numbers.

KINDERGARTEN PLACE VALUE

In kindergarten students should have several opportunities to work with the teen numbers (see Figure 6.2). They should do this from the concrete, through the pictorial to the abstract level. Too often, text books spend a day on each number and then before we know it the unit is finished. It is important to have ongoing practice and to address the fact that students don't learn everything they need to know about the number 11 in one day. This is where a workstation can be so helpful because now you can have a whole set of activities around exploring different teen numbers separately and together.

Figure 6.2 Examples of Concrete, Pictorial and Abstract Activities

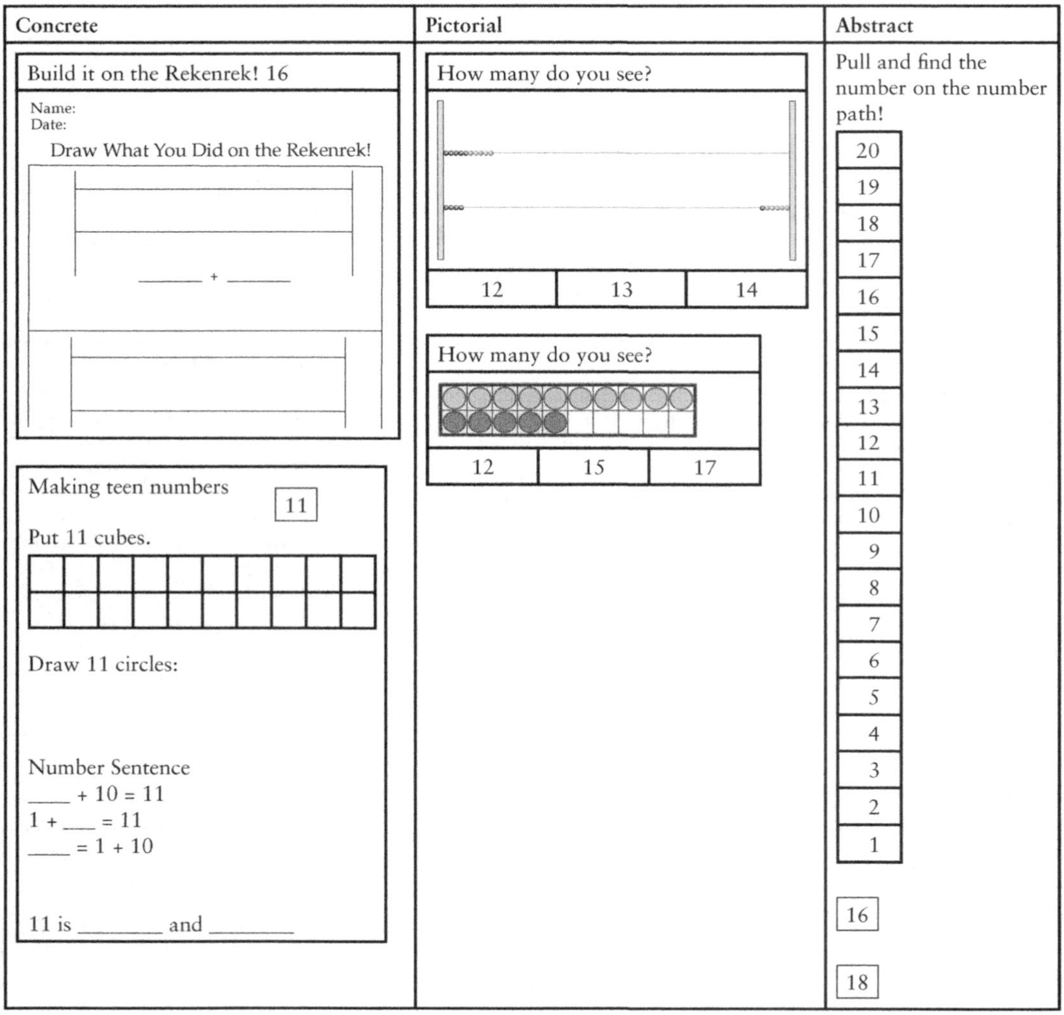

Concrete	Pictorial	Abstract
Build it on the Rekenrek! 16 Name: Date: Draw What You Did on the Rekenrek! _____ + _____ **Making teen numbers** [11] Put 11 cubes. Draw 11 circles: Number Sentence ____ + 10 = 11 1 + ___ = 11 ____ = 1 + 10 11 is _____ and _____	**How many do you see?** | 12 | 13 | 14 | **How many do you see?** | 12 | 15 | 17 |	Pull and find the number on the number path! 20 19 18 17 16 15 14 13 12 11 10 9 8 7 6 5 4 3 2 1 [16] [18]

KINDERGARTEN COMPARING NUMBERS

There are several really important ideas about comparing numbers and scaffolding that work in the workstation. When comparing numbers, students should go through a cycle of matching and then counting and then using their mental number line (see Figures 6.3–6.5). All of these activities are based on students understanding place value. Students start by comparing numbers within 10. Then, they should move up to comparing numbers within 20.

In kindergarten, students learn to compare numbers within 10. I would place this in the place value center because it is continued all the way through the grades. The basic framework of comparing by matching and then counting and then using the mental number line and an understanding of place and value of the numbers is continued throughout all the grades.

Framework for Teaching Comparison at Any Level

Figure 6.3 Comparison

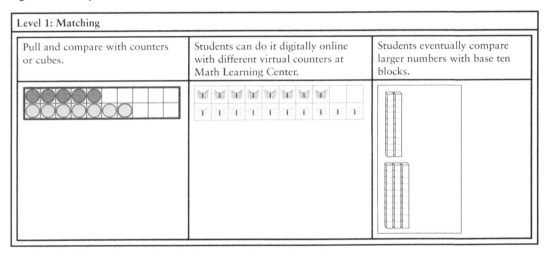

Level 1: Matching		
Pull and compare with counters or cubes.	Students can do it digitally online with different virtual counters at Math Learning Center.	Students eventually compare larger numbers with base ten blocks.

Figure 6.4 Comparison

Level 2: Counting

Counting on a number path. Students pull a card and place their marker on that card. Their partner does the same. Whoever is farthest along on the number line wins a point. Whoever gets 10 points first wins.

1	2	3	4	5	6	7	8	9	10	11	12	13	14	15	16	17	18	19	20

Hundred grid

1	2	3	4	5	6	7	8	9	10
11	12	13	14	15	16	17	18	19	20
21	22	23	24	25	26	27	28	29	30
31	32	33	34	35	36	37	38	39	40
41	42	43	44	45	46	47	48	49	50
51	52	53	54	55	56	57	58	59	60
61	62	63	64	65	66	67	68	69	70
71	72	73	74	75	76	77	78	79	80
81	82	83	84	85	86	87	88	89	90
91	92	93	94	95	96	97	98	99	100

Figure 6.5 Comparison

Level 3: Mental Number Line
Mental Number Line
Card game

2	5
77	32

In kindergarten students work with comparing numbers between 10 and 20 (see Figures 6.6 and 6.7) (depending on the state).

Figure 6.6 Work Within 10

Concrete	Pictorial	Abstract
Students use a double ten frame. They then pull a card and compare counters on it. 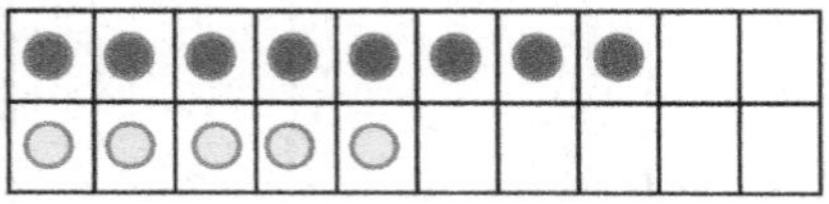	Students pull a number card. They each color that many squares. One person colors the top and the other person colors the bottom. Whoever has the most wins that round. They do it four times. Whoever wins the most rounds wins the game. 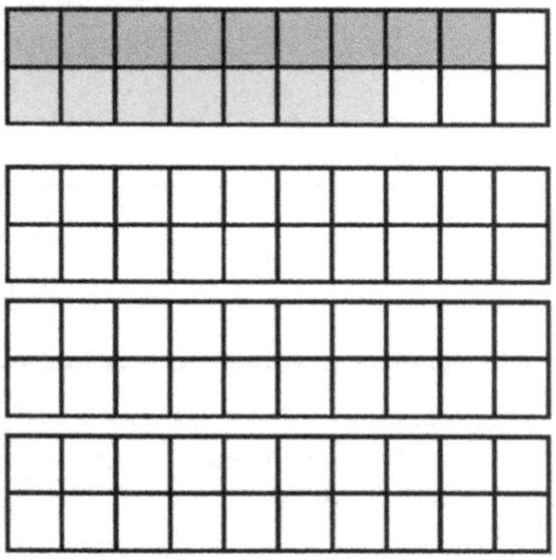	Students can play card games where they pull a card and compare the numbers using a mental number line and their understanding of place and value. 9 7

Figure 6.7 More Comparison Activities

More or Less Activities

Students pull cards and they have to count how many they each have. The student that has the most says, "I have more." The student who has more cubes on their card gets to keep both the cards. When all the cards are gone they count the cards to see who has the most cards. Whoever has the most cards is the winner.

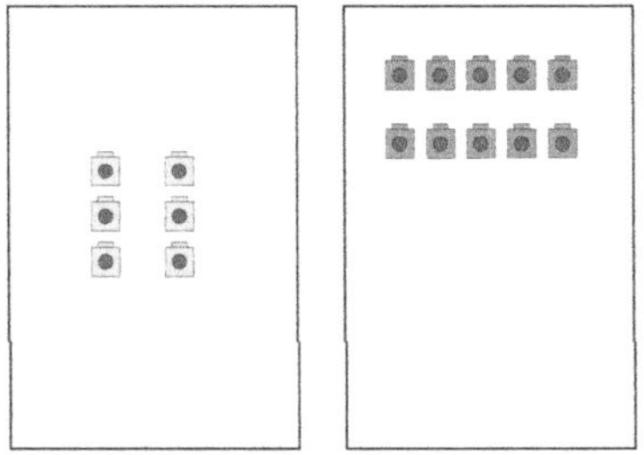

Students can also work either concretely or digitally to do this as well.
Online Number Frames from Math Learning Center

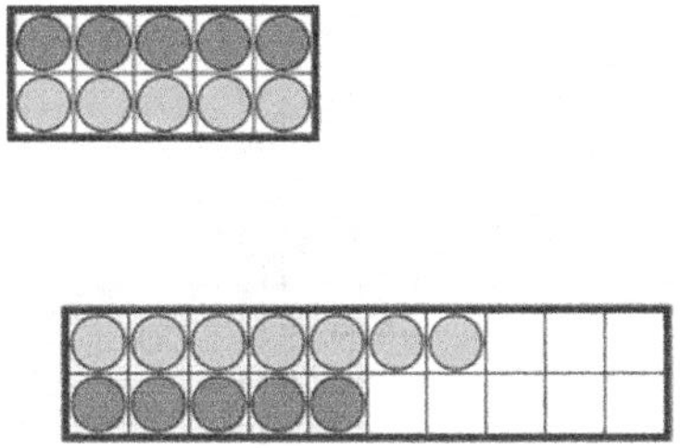

Online Rekenrek from Math Learning Center

Each child pulls a number. They then build a cube tower of that number. They then compare their towers. Then, they color their towers.

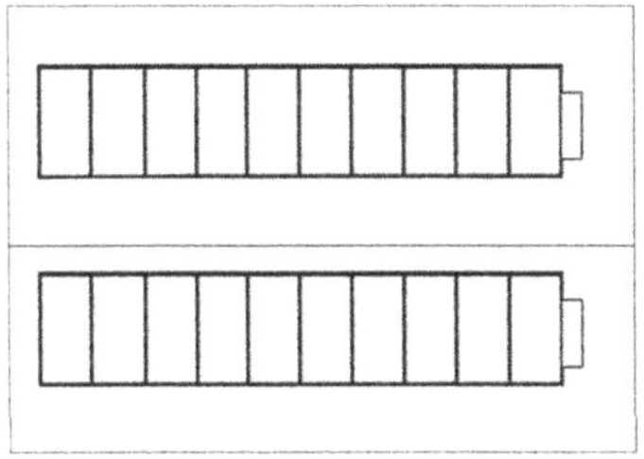

They should have a language frame that says:

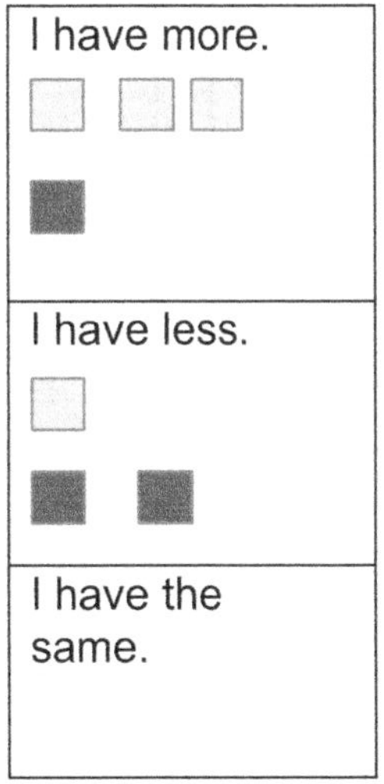

I have more.

I have less.

I have the same.

Students play a board game. In the game they have to cover either **one more or one less.**

5	7	3	6
8	9	10	2
2	4	7	8

Cover 1 more than 5.	Cover 1 less than 3.	Cover 1 more than 4.	Cover 1 less than 5.

Work With 20 (see Figures 6.8 and 6.9)

Students should pull a number and then build it in the double ten frame and then circle or put a square around their number. In this way they can see it visually with a model and also abstractly on the number line. Where appropriate, students can compare with the symbol. In the workstation, there should be a language frame to scaffold student talk. For example:

Figure 6.8 More Comparison Activities

_____ is less than _____	<
_____ is more than _____	>
_____ is the same as _____	=

Figure 6.9 Activities to Show Comparison

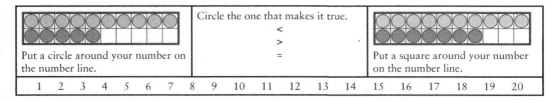

Use comparative language to describe two numbers up to 20 presented as written numerals: Before or after, more or less, greater or smaller, equal, more or fewer.

Generate a number that is one more than or one less than another number up to at least 20 (see Figure 6.10).

Figure 6.10 Before and After Activities

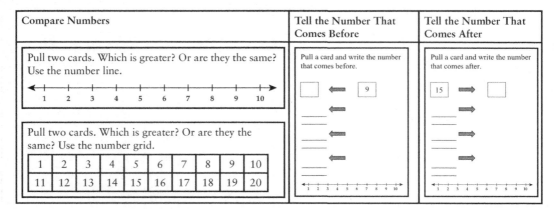

FIRST GRADE PLACE VALUE

In first grade, all of the place value standards are major cluster or priority standards depending on your state. Students should have the year to explore them and own the concepts. It is so important because it lays the foundation for second grade and multi-digit calculations. Students should have the opportunity to work with these concepts concretely, pictorially and abstractly often, independently, with partners and in small groups. Many of the workstations are done as whole class routines in the beginning and then transitioned into workstations later on. Place value is not only a unit of study but also one of the four must-have workstations that stays up throughout the year.

In first grade, students are supposed to pick up where kindergarten left off. In most states, this is at the number 20. The reality is that many students coming into first grade do not have a robust understanding of numbers within 20. So it is really important to set up place value workstations that review numbers within 20 for the first few months of school. For some students, you might even have to leave these stations up longer. As you begin to teach place value, you will add to the first grade workstation.

Extending the Counting Sequence

At this level students are expected to learn to count within 120 (see Figure 6.11). They are required to be able to read, write and represent a number of objects with a written numeral. Although many states do not require that students be able to read or write number words at this stage, I believe that they should know how to recognize their number words at least through ten and possibly through twenty.

Figure 6.11 Representing Numbers

	Concrete	Pictorial	Abstract
Read and Represent Numbers			
In these type of activities students should be able to read/recognize a number. They know the name and can say it. These activities are usually coupled with reading the number and representing it.	It could be that students have to pull a card and show that number on the rekenrek or with counters on ten frames. You could also use swim noodles cut into longs and shorts so the students have to represent the 10s and 1s in this way.	They pull a card and do a base ten sketch. 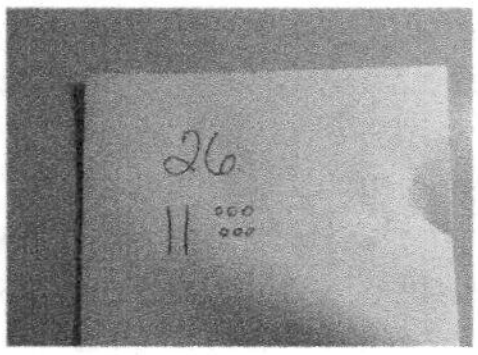 26 11 They pull a clip card and have to determine how many 10s and 1s are represented. 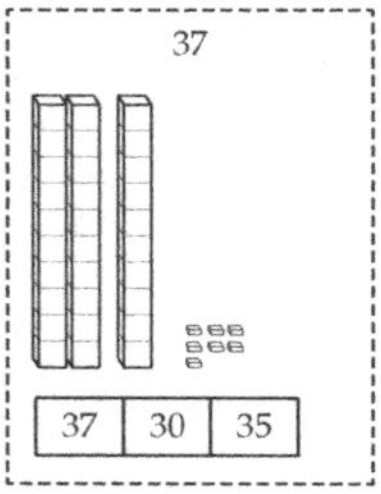 37 37 | 30 | 35	Students can match pictures with numbers. 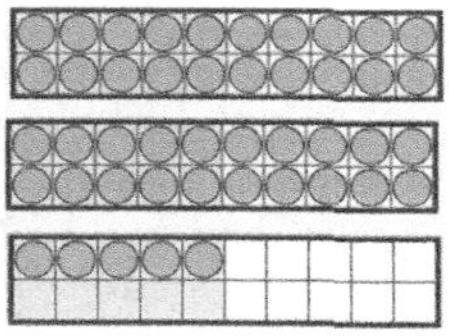 45
Write Numbers	Number: 32 Write it: _____ _____ _____ **Hundred Grid** 	1	2	3	4	5	6	7	8	9	10
11	12	13	14	15	16	17	18	19	20
21	22	23	24	25	26	27	28	29	30
31	32	33	34	35	36	37	38	39	40
41	42	43	44	45	46	47	48	49	50
51	52	53	54	55	56	57	58	59	60
61	62	63	64	65	66	67	68	69	70
71	72	73	74	75	76	77	78	79	80
81	82	83	84	85	86	87	88	89	90
91	92	93	94	95	96	97	98	99	100 | **Base Ten Sketch: Use lines and dots** **Ten Frame** Circle the number: 1 2 3 4 5 6 7 8 9 10 11 12 13 14 15 16 17 18 19 20 21 22 23 24 25 26 27 28 29 30 31 32 33 34 35 36 37 38 39 40 Before Number After		

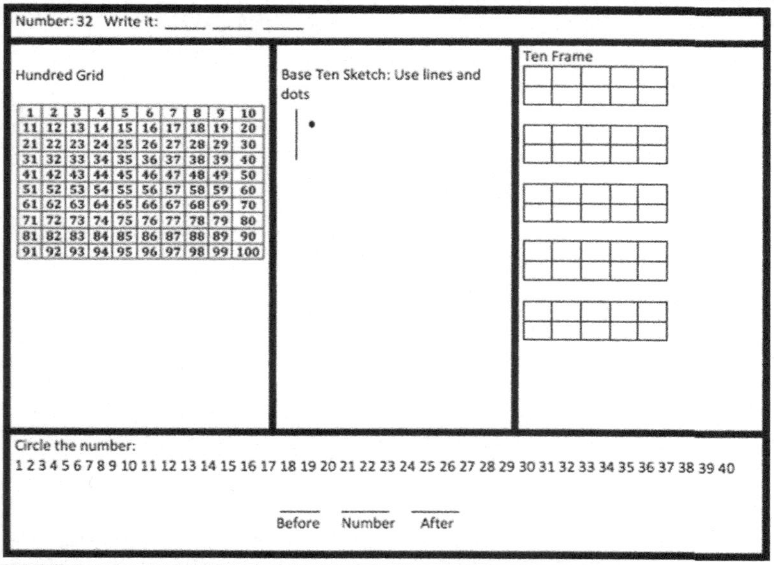

UNDERSTANDING THE BASE TEN SYSTEM (SEE FIGURE 6.12)

Figure 6.12 Base Ten System

Concrete		
Students should have plenty of opportunities to work with bundling 10s and 1s. They need to build their own understanding of 10s and 1s before we give them a pre-made system of base ten blocks. Students can also pick a card and build the number. **Build it!** 28 || ▢▢▢ ▢▢▢ ▢	**Craft Sticks, Popsicle Sticks or Straws** For example, students might work with bundling popsicle sticks. In a workstation a student might have to pick a number and then show that number with bundles of sticks. They would bundle a group of ten sticks for a 10 and the loose sticks would be the 1s. Another example is building tens and ones with bean sticks. Students would glue 10 beans on a stick to make a 10 and the loose ones would be 1s. To make 100 the students lay out ten sticks and then lay crisscross 10 bean sticks on top of them to make a raft.	**Beans and Cups** Students can also work with beans and cups. Students would put ten beans in every cup and the loose ones on the side.

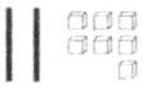

Teaching Place Value with Cups

It is really important for students to be able to construct their understanding of place value by working with different objects. Here are a few ideas:

Red Solo Cups for Place Value
www.youtube.com/watch?v=xkx2OKuPYeo
www.youtube.com/watch?v=nzy4wCIBB_I
www.bargainblessings.com/interactive-childrens-math-activities-for-summertime/

Pictorial		
	Number: 32 Write it: ____ ____ ____ Hundred Grid Base Ten Sketch: Use lines and dots Ten Frame Circle the number: 1 2 3 4 5 6 7 8 9 10 11 12 13 14 15 16 17 18 19 20 21 22 23 24 25 26 27 28 29 30 31 32 33 34 35 36 37 38 39 40 Before Number After	Students have to pick a card and sketch the number with base ten blocks. Sketch it! 28

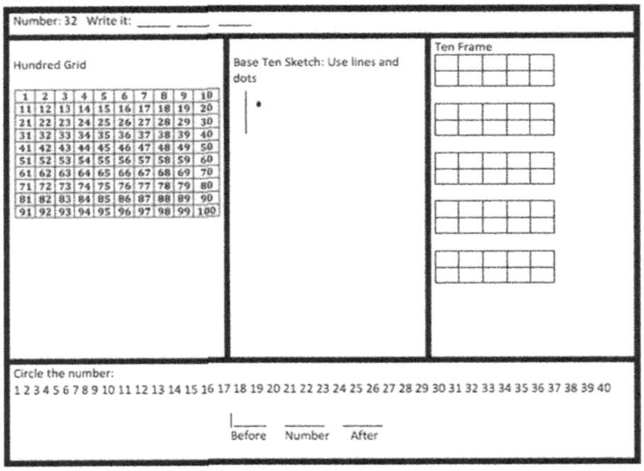

Abstract		
	Students have to pull two cards and make the largest number possible. Whoever has the largest number gets to keep the cards. Students should record their work. Whoever has the most cards after five rounds wins. | Cards	Recording Sheet
---	---
9 4	P1 P2 ____ . ____ ____ ____ ____ ____		**Place value bingo** Students each have their own bingo cards and they pull a card and cover the space on their bingo card that matches the game card. two 10s and four 1s | 23	97	35	81
---	---	---	---
42	74	59	16
99	80	56	38
44	24	67	11	

FIRST GRADE: REPRESENTING NUMBERS

Along with building understanding of 10s and 1s, first graders also learn a variety of ways to represent a number. They need several opportunities throughout the year to practice composing and decomposing numbers, representing numbers pictorially, using the expanded form as well as the standard form. Most states don't introduce the expanded form until second grade; however, Texas and a few other states introduce it in first grade. Nevertheless, first grade covers a big number range and so I suggest breaking it up into parts so students can feel a sense of success along the journey. Maybe the first part of the workstation is a review of K, the second part is representing numbers through 50 and then the third part would be representing the numbers through 120 (see Figure 6.13).

Figure 6.13 Representing Numbers

| Objects Composing and Decomposing Numbers. It is important that students have ongoing opportunities to practice representing numbers in a variety of ways. | Beaded Number Line 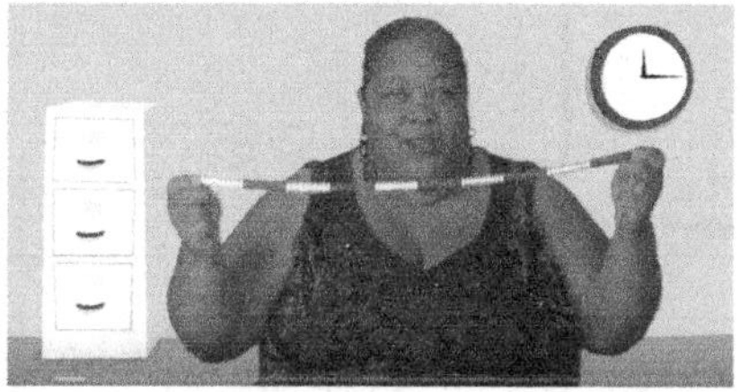 | Base Ten Blocks 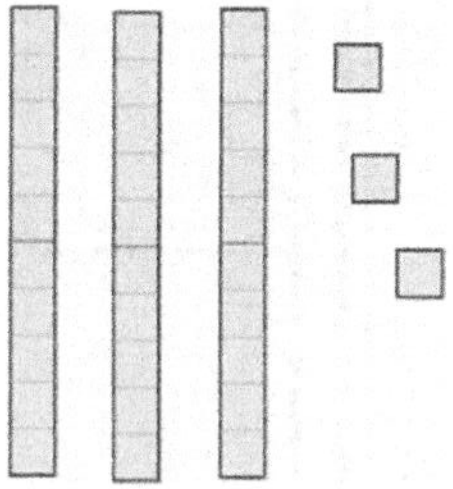 | Part-Part Whole Mats 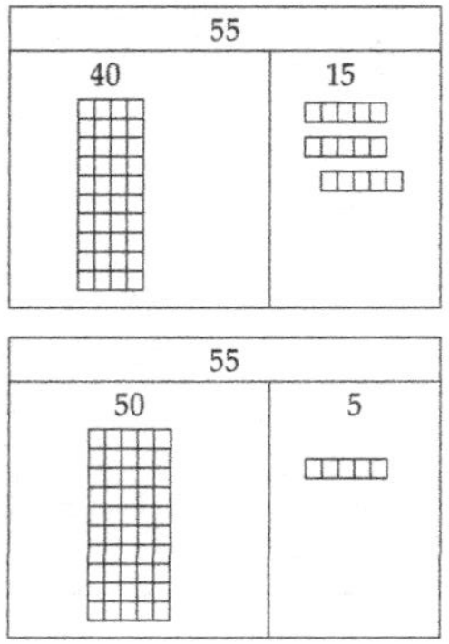 |
| Pictorial Students should do base ten sketches and ten frame fill-ins. | Base Ten Sketches 25 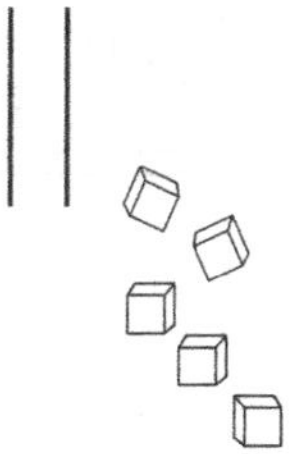 | | Ten Frame Fill-ins 58 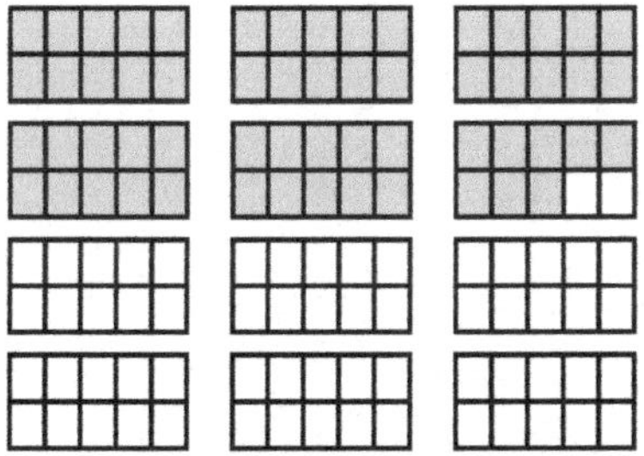 |

Expanded

Students should definitely be working with expanded form cards.

60

2

Board Game where students work on expanded form and other representations

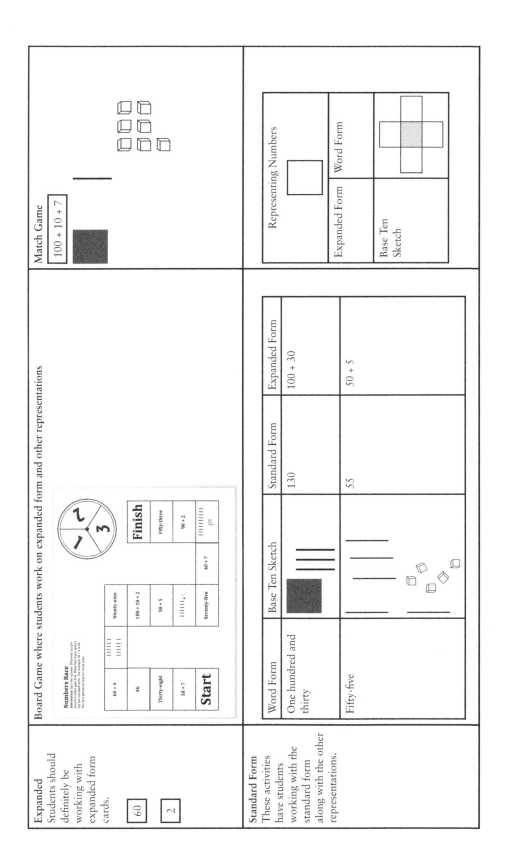

Numbers Race

Each person takes a turn on the spinner. Whoever has the fourth number goes first. Move that many spaces. Say the standard form. For example 60 + 4 is 64. The first person to land on finish wins.

60 + 4												Ninety-nine
46		100 + 10 + 2
Thirty-eight		50 + 5
10 + 7							Seventy-five
Start		40 + 7

Finish — Fifty-three — 90 + 2

Match Game

100 + 10 + 7

Representing Numbers

Expanded Form	Word Form
Base Ten Sketch	

Standard Form

These activities have students working with the standard form along with the other representations.

Word Form	Base Ten Sketch	Standard Form	Expanded Form
One hundred and thirty		130	100 + 30
Fifty-five		55	50 + 5

FIRST GRADE: COMPARING NUMBERS

First graders worked with 10s and 1s in kindergarten with the teen numbers. They need to also build on their understanding from kindergarten of the teen numbers, meaning they should understand that teen numbers are a 10 and some 1s. So this should be up and running in the place value workstation from the beginning of the year from first grade. Students should see this as an ongoing conversation. It is a continuation of what they have been learning, not something brand new. The more connections we can make for our students the better. At this grade students are expected to understand that the two digits of a two-digit number represent 10s and 1s. They need to understand that ten 1s can be represented as a ten. They also are expected to understand the meaning of 10s (that two 10s is 20 and three 10s is 30, etc.)

The first grade aspect of this station is that students should be comparing two two-digit numbers based on the meaning of the 10s and one digits (see Figures 6.14–6.16). Moreover, students should be able to compare these numbers with the symbols >, =, and <. I would sequence this so students start with comparing numbers to 20 and then to 50 and then to 80 and then 100 and then 120. So, it should be a gradual progression. There shouldn't be this rush to use the symbols. Students should have a lot of opportunities to use and understand the vocabulary with scaffolded cards so they can work with the ideas of greater than, less than and the same as, etc. There is a great deal of vocabulary involved with this concept that must be built and owned. Before there is an emphasis on the symbols, there should be a focus on the comparative language. This language should be heard every day during calendar when students are working with the daily graphs.

Figure 6.14 Working Within 120 Using Symbols >, <, or =

Concrete	Pictorial	Abstract
Each partner pulls a card. Each partner builds the number with base ten blocks. Whoever has the largest number gets to take a counter and put it on their ten frame. Whoever gets ten counters first wins.	Students pull a card and draw a base ten sketch. Whoever has the largest number gets to take a counter and put it on their ten frame. Whoever gets ten counters first wins.	Students pull two cards and compare the numbers. Whoever has the highest number wins a point. Whoever gets to five points first wins. They should have to record their work on an activity sheet for accountability purposes.

Students can also build and compare numbers on the rekenrek. Each student would use their own rekenrek and then whoever has more has to explain why they have more. In first grade students should have rekenreks that go to 20 and also ones that go to 100. You can buy them or build them with the students. 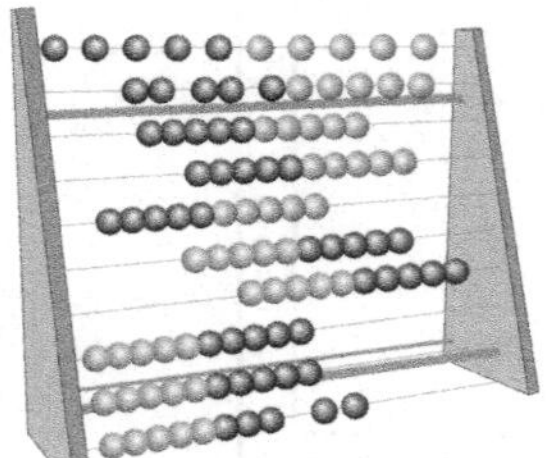	Students pull a base ten flashcard and compare their numbers. Whoever has the largest number gets to take a counter and put it on their ten frame. Whoever gets ten counters first wins. 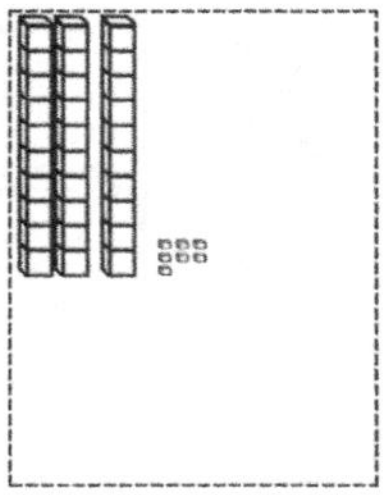 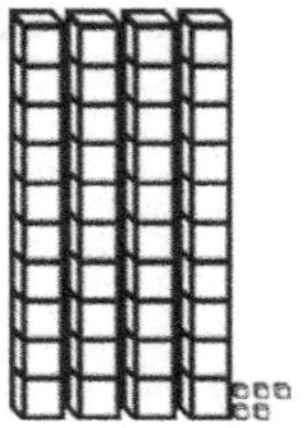	Both of these are abstract practice cards. They can be self-checking because the answer is on the back. Students should have to explain their thinking to their partner. The first card is more of a DOK level 1 and the second one can be a DOK level if it requires explanation.
		
		1. Which statement is true?
		
		    A. 54 < 24
		    B. 35 > 29
		    C. 67 < 29
		
		Compare the numbers
		
		52 ☐ 37
		
		> | < | =

Figure 6.15 Generate a Number That Is Greater Than or Less Than a Given Whole Number Up to 120

In all of these cases students would pull a number or roll a number or spin a number and then do some activity to find a number that is greater than or less than the starter number. To determine if they were looking for a number that is greater than or less than the original number they could pull a card or spin a spinner.

Concrete

Build it cards! Students pull an equation and build it with a rekenrek. So if students pull a 29, then they have to build a number that is greater than that on the rekenrek.

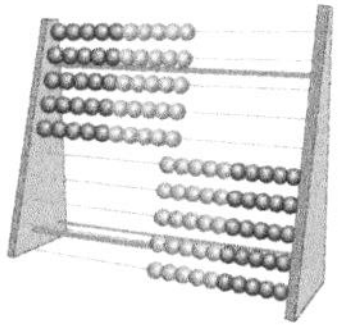

Build a number on the rekenrek greater than 29.

Build it cards! Students pull an equation and build it with base ten blocks. If students pull a 50 they have to build a number that is greater than that with the base ten blocks.

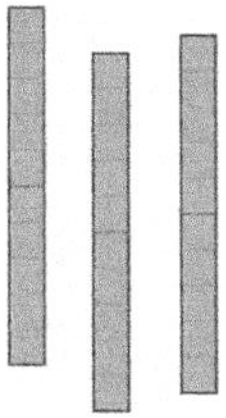

Build a number with the base ten blocks smaller than 50.

Pictorial

Students pull a card that has instructions. Then, they have to write the starter number and follow the directions. Students have to do a base ten sketch.

Sketch a number that is less than 30.

Students pull a card that has instructions. Then, they have to write the starter number and follow the directions. Students have to do a base ten sketch.

Sketch a number that is more than 25

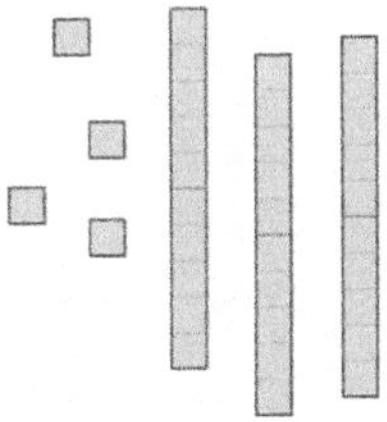

Abstract

Students pull a number and they have to find a number on the number grid that is greater than or less than the number they pulled.

1	2	3	4	5	6	7	8	9	10
11	12	13	14	15	16	17	18	19	20
21	22	23	24	25	26	27	28	29	30
31	32	33	34	35	36	37	38	39	40
41	42	43	44	45	46	47	48	49	50
51	52	53	54	55	56	57	58	59	60
61	62	63	64	65	66	67	68	69	70
71	72	73	74	75	76	77	78	79	80
81	82	83	84	85	86	87	88	89	90
91	92	93	94	95	96	97	98	99	100

Students can play four in a row.
They pull a card and follow the instructions. Whoever gets four in a row covered first wins. For example:

Cover a number that is greater than 50.

34	57	99	120
45	11	8	49
72	29	110	100
91	63	80	77

They can use the hundred grid as a scaffold.

1	2	3	4	5	6	7	8	9	10
11	12	13	14	15	16	17	18	19	20
21	22	23	24	25	26	27	28	29	30
31	32	33	34	35	36	37	38	39	40
41	42	43	44	45	46	47	48	49	50
51	52	53	54	55	56	57	58	59	60
61	62	63	64	65	66	67	68	69	70
71	72	73	74	75	76	77	78	79	80
81	82	83	84	85	86	87	88	89	90
91	92	93	94	95	96	97	98	99	100

Figure 6.16 Order Whole Numbers Up to 120 Using Place Value and Open Number Lines

Pictorial Students would use pictorial models to order numbers.	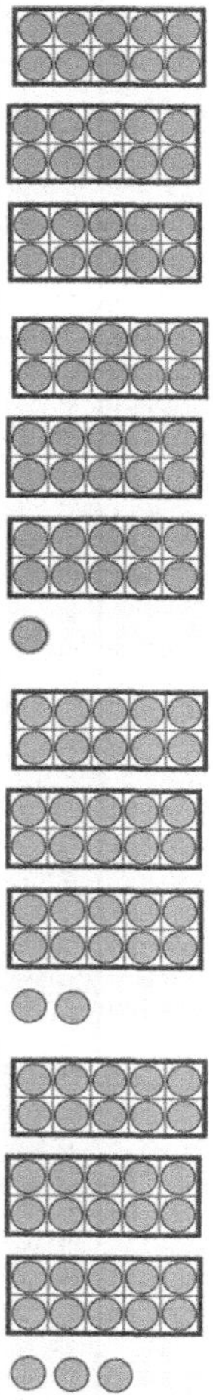
Abstract Students would work with hundred grid puzzles and number lines to order numbers.	21, 22 __, 24, __ __ 35, __, __, 39, __ __ 42 __ 43 __ 45 __ __ 50 __ __ 53, 54 __ __

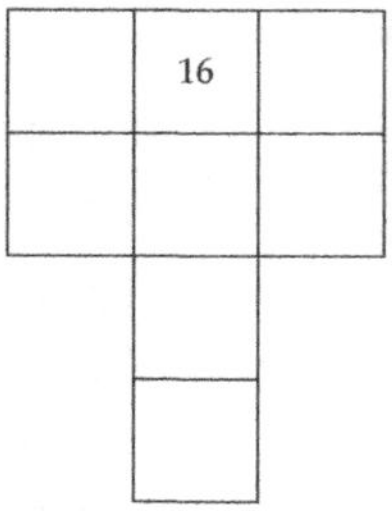

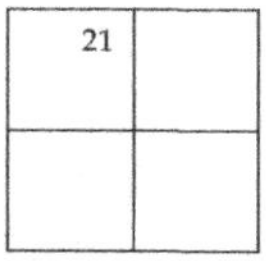

USE PLACE VALUE UNDERSTANDING AND PROPERTIES OF OPERATIONS TO ADD AND SUBTRACT

At this level, students are adding within 100 (see Figure 6.17). They are expected to add a two-digit number and a one-digit number. They are expected to add a two-digit number and a multiple of 10. They are expected to be using concrete models or drawings and strategies based in place value, properties of operations and/or the relationship between addition and subtraction. Students should be able to relate the strategy to a written method and explain the reasoning used. Students are expected to use different strategies to add 10s and 10s and 1s and 1s.

Figure 6.17 Adding a Two-Digit Number and a One-Digit Number

Concrete: Use the Base Ten Blocks	Pictorial: Use Base Ten Sketches	Abstract: Use Abstract Scaffolds (the Hundred Grid Is a Scaffold to This)
Build it cards! Students pull an equation and build it with a rekenrek. 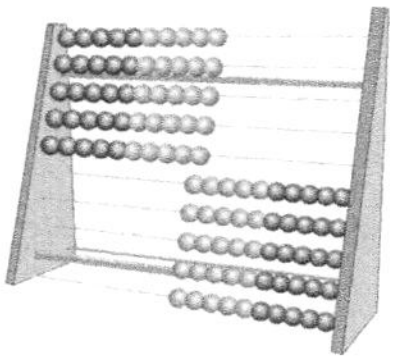	Students match a flashcard and an equation. 34 + 8 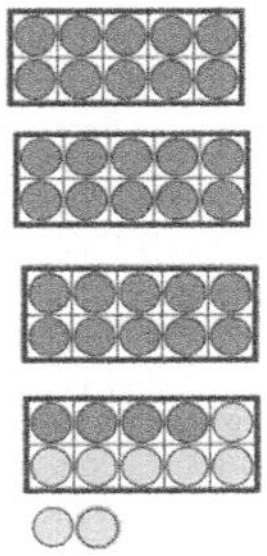 Students practice with clip cards: 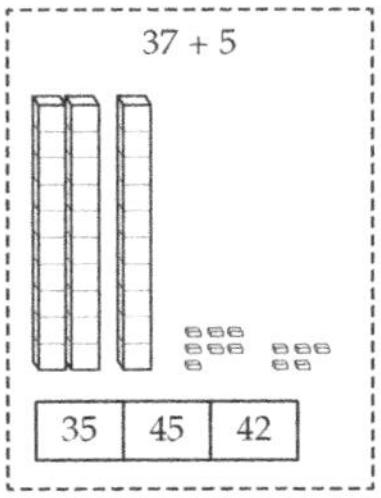 37 + 5 35 45 42	Students can also use the hundred grid to count up.
Build it cards! Students pull an equation and build it with base ten blocks. Using two different colors helps to scaffold student understanding.	Pull and Sketch. Students pull an equation and sketch it. 24 + 5 Pull a card. Sketch the equation.	Use hundred grids without the numbers.

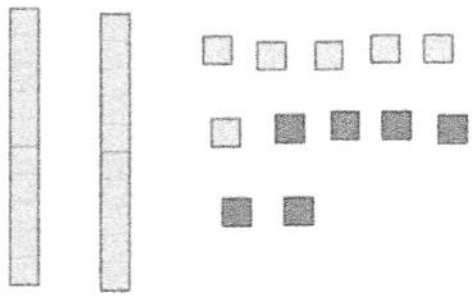

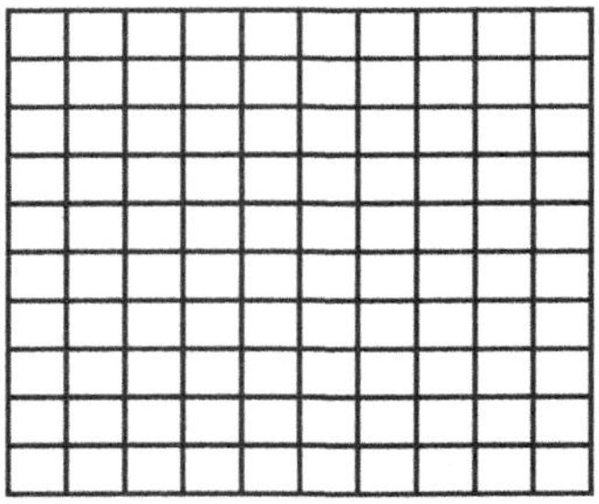

The hundred grid contains:

1	2	3	4	5	6	7	8	9	10
11	12	13	14	15	16	17	18	19	20
21	22	23	24	25	26	27	28	29	30
31	32	33	34	35	36	37	38	39	40
41	42	43	44	45	46	47	48	49	50
51	52	53	54	55	56	57	58	59	60
61	62	63	64	65	66	67	68	69	70
71	72	73	74	75	76	77	78	79	80
81	82	83	84	85	86	87	88	89	90
91	92	93	94	95	96	97	98	99	100

STATION E: MENTALLY FINDING TEN MORE OR TEN LESS (SEE FIGURE 6.18)

At this level, students are expected when given a two-digit number to mentally find ten more or ten less than the number, without having to count. Moreover, they are expected to be able to explain their reasoning. I think it is really important for students to have ample opportunity to understand this concept before doing it abstractly. It is a very difficult concept and some first graders struggle intensely with it. I would argue that it must be built from the concrete, through the pictorial to the abstract.

Figure 6.18 Activities for Ten More or Ten Less

Concrete: Use the Base Ten blocks	Pictorial: Use Base Ten Sketches	Abstract: Use the Mental Number Line (the Hundred Grid Is a Scaffold to This)
Build it cards! Students pull an equation and build it with a rekenrek. 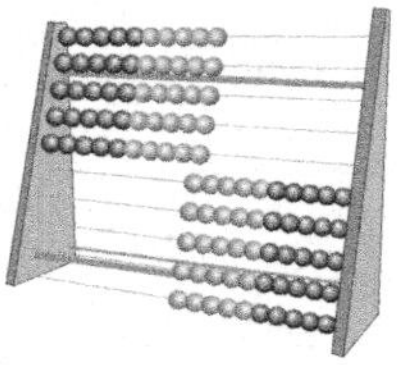	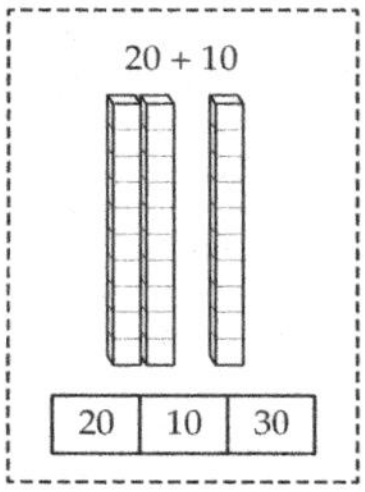	At first students might use the hundred grid to help scaffold their thinking but eventually they have to just pull a flashcard and state the number that comes next.
Build it cards! Students pull an equation and build it with base ten blocks. Using two different colors helps to scaffold the idea.	Pull and Sketch. Students pull an equation and sketch it. 20 + 10 / Pull a card. Sketch the equation. / Also students should work with number grid puzzles.	Students pull a flashcard and have to know what is ten more by using place value. The cards are self-checking because the answer is on the back. 20 + 10 30 / Student can also play a board game.

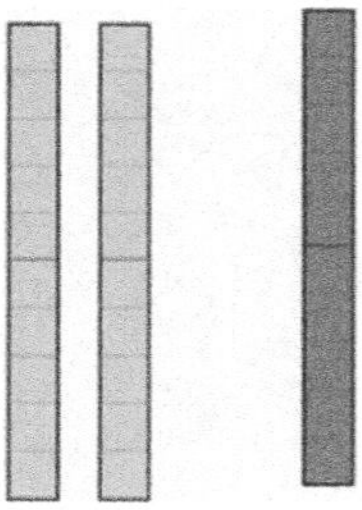

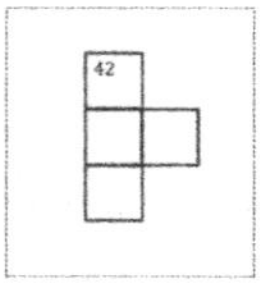

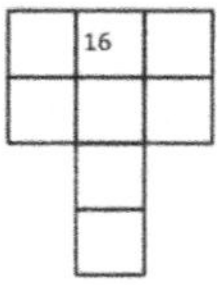

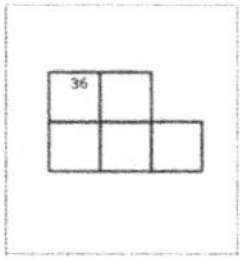

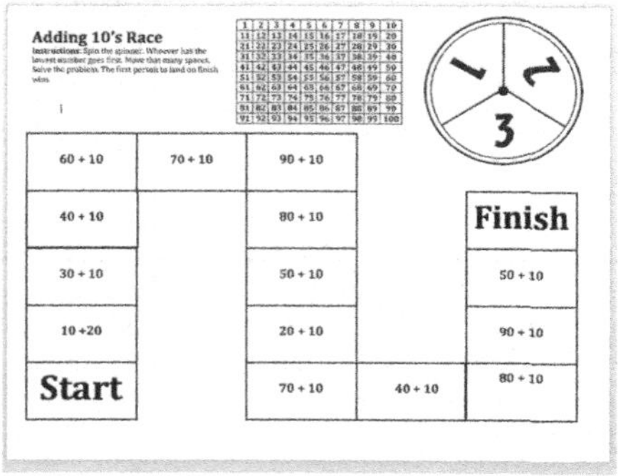

STATION F1: ADD MULTIPLES OF 10 (SEE FIGURE 6.19)

At this level, students are expected to add multiples of 10 in the range of 10–90 from multiples of 10 in the range of 10–90 (positive or zero differences) using concrete models, drawings or strategies based on place value, properties of operations and/or the relationship between addition and subtraction; relate the strategy to a written method and explain the reasoning used. In terms of leveling, you want students to first work on concrete activities, then pictorial and then abstract.

Figure 6.19 Activities for Adding Multiples of 10

Concrete: Use the Base Ten Blocks	Pictorial: Use Base Ten Sketches	Abstract: Use the Mental Number Line (the Hundred Grid Is a Scaffold to This)
Build it cards! Students pull an equation and build it with a rekenrek or base ten blocks. 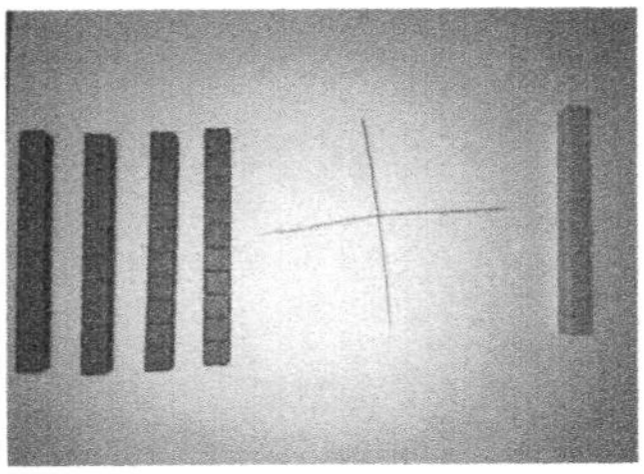	Students might practice adding 10s on a clip card. 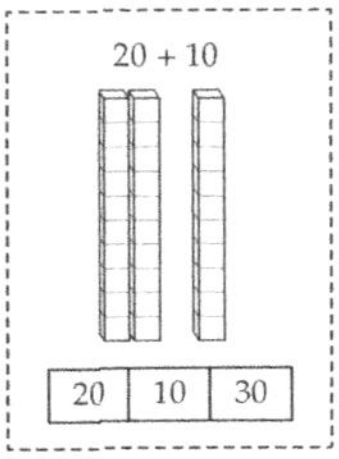 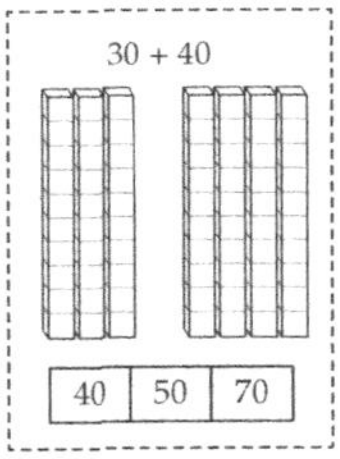 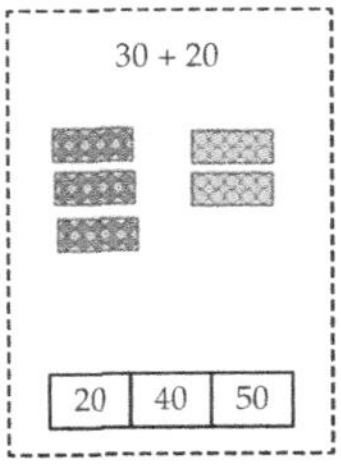	At first students might use the hundred grid to help scaffold their thinking but eventually they have to just pull a flashcard and state the number that comes next.
Build it cards! Students pull an equation and build it with base ten blocks.	Pull and Sketch. Students pull an equation and sketch it. 20 + 20 Pull a card. Sketch the equation.	Students pull a flashcard and have to know what is 10 or more by using place value. The cards are self-checking because the answer is on the back. 20 + 30 50

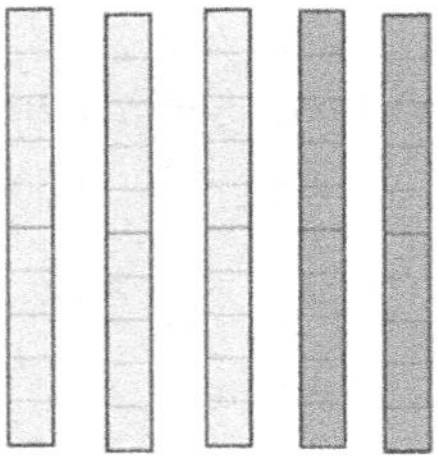

STATION F2: SUBTRACT MULTIPLES OF 10 (SEE FIGURE 6.20)

At this level, students are expected to subtract multiples of 10 in the range of 10–90 from multiples of 10 in the range of 10–90 (positive or zero differences) using concrete models, drawings or strategies based on place value, properties of operations and/or the relationship between addition and subtraction; relate the strategy to a written method and explain the reasoning used. In terms of leveling, you want students to first work on concrete activities, then pictorial and then abstract.

Figure 6.20 Activities for Subtracting Multiples of 10

Concrete Using Base 10 Blocks	Pictorial Drawings At the Pictorial Level the Scaffolding Is Visual	Abstract There Are No Visual Scaffolds
Students use the base ten blocks to build the equation. 30 – 10 = 20 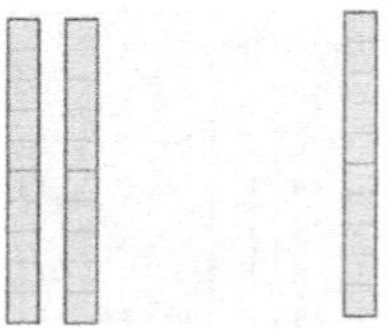 	Students might practice subtracting 10s on a clip card. 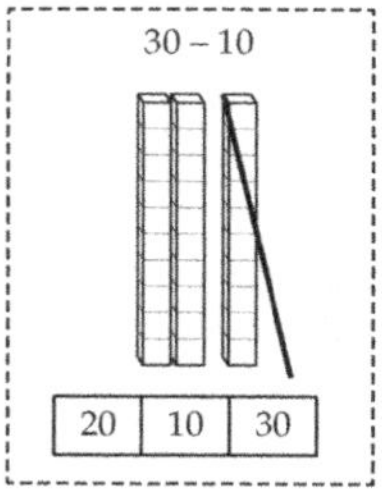 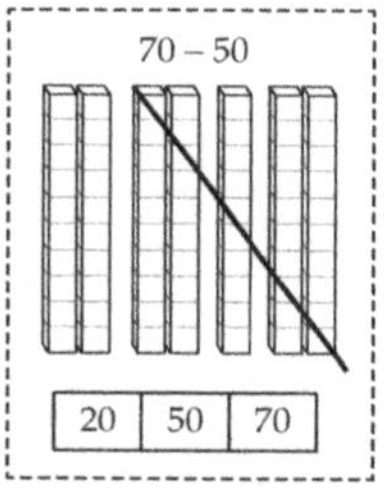 30 – 10 20 | 10 | 30 70 – 50 20 | 50 | 70	At first students might use the hundred grid to help scaffold their thinking but eventually they should be able to pull a card and state the difference.
Students use the rekenrek to solve the equation. 	Students play a match game with visuals and a number sentence. 30 – 10 = 20 	Students pull a flashcard and have to know the difference. The cards are self-checking because the answer is on the back. 50 – 30 20

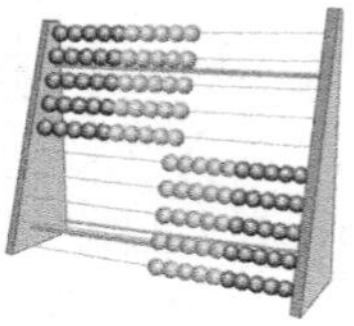

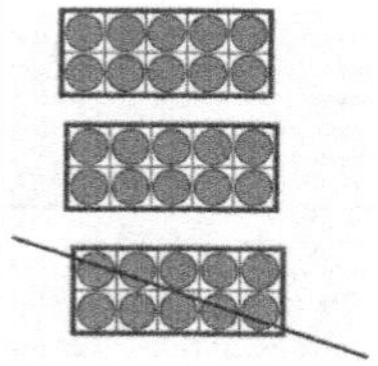

   Use concrete and pictorial models to determine the sum of a multiple of 10 and a one-digit number in problems up to 99 (see Figures 6.21 and 6.22).

Figure 6.21 More Multiple of 10 Activities

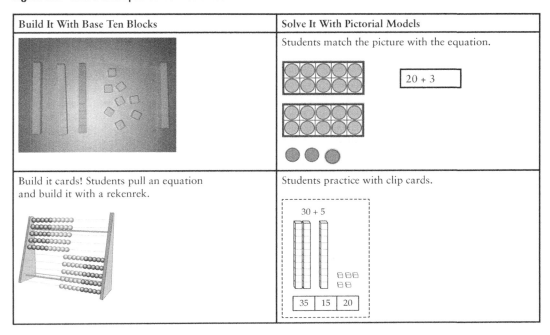

Build It With Base Ten Blocks	Solve It With Pictorial Models
	Students match the picture with the equation. 20 + 3
Build it cards! Students pull an equation and build it with a rekenrek.	Students practice with clip cards. 30 + 5 35 15 20

Figure 6.22 More Multiple of 10 Activities

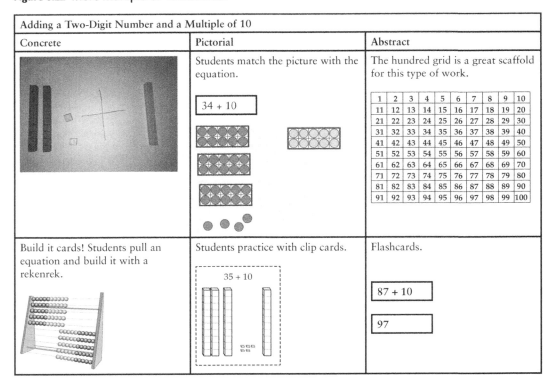

Adding a Two-Digit Number and a Multiple of 10		
Concrete	Pictorial	Abstract
	Students match the picture with the equation. 34 + 10	The hundred grid is a great scaffold for this type of work. 1 2 3 4 5 6 7 8 9 10 11 12 13 14 15 16 17 18 19 20 21 22 23 24 25 26 27 28 29 30 31 32 33 34 35 36 37 38 39 40 41 42 43 44 45 46 47 48 49 50 51 52 53 54 55 56 57 58 59 60 61 62 63 64 65 66 67 68 69 70 71 72 73 74 75 76 77 78 79 80 81 82 83 84 85 86 87 88 89 90 91 92 93 94 95 96 97 98 99 100
Build it cards! Students pull an equation and build it with a rekenrek.	Students practice with clip cards. 35 + 10	Flashcards. 87 + 10 97

SECOND GRADE PLACE VALUE

Second grade place value is fundamental to learning math. It wraps up those beginning foundations of number. By the end of second grade students are supposed to be completely fluent in knowing about place and value of numbers within 1000 and adding and subtracting numbers within 100. Even though they add and subtract within 1000, the fluency is within 100.

Students need a variety of experiences working with manipulatives to build conceptual understanding of place value. It is sequential. We can't just skip steps when students are shaky. We have to build firm foundations and so the first grade stations are an integral part of the second grade stations. Some students will take some time to master those first grade skills that are shaky and they need to be given that time to practice. This doesn't mean that we don't go ahead and discuss and explore the second grade standards but it does mean that we also give those students who need it, the extra help and practice with the prior standards.

Second Grade Leveled Place Value Workstations (see Figures 6.23 and 6.24)

Figure 6.23 Second Grade Place Value

State Standards
First Part: Understanding Place and Value

- Understand that the three digits of a three-digit number represent amounts of 100s, 10s and 1s; e.g., 706 equals 7 100s, 0 10s, and 6 1s. Understand the following as special cases: 100 can be thought of as a bundle of ten 10s—called a "hundred."
- Use concrete and pictorial models to compose and decompose numbers up to 1200 in more than one way as a sum of so many 1000s, 100s, 10s and 1s.
- Students should be able to read and write numbers to 1000 or 1200 (depending on the state).

Figure 6.24 Place Value Activities

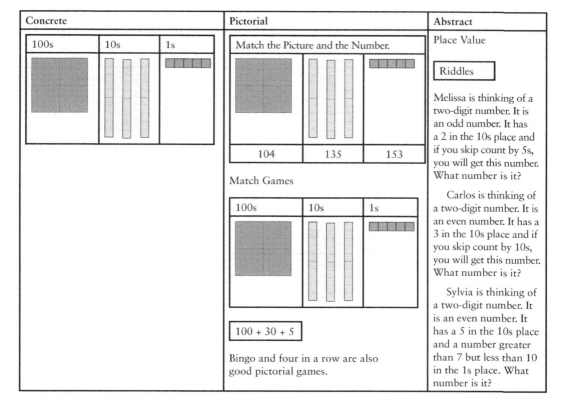

Concrete	Pictorial	Abstract
100s 10s 1s	Match the Picture and the Number. 104 135 153	Place Value **Riddles** Melissa is thinking of a two-digit number. It is an odd number. It has a 2 in the 10s place and if you skip count by 5s, you will get this number. What number is it?
	Match Games 100s 10s 1s 100 + 30 + 5 Bingo and four in a row are also good pictorial games.	Carlos is thinking of a two-digit number. It is an even number. It has a 3 in the 10s place and if you skip count by 10s, you will get this number. What number is it? Sylvia is thinking of a two-digit number. It is an even number. It has a 5 in the 10s place and a number greater than 7 but less than 10 in the 1s place. What number is it?

Figure 6.25 Representing Numbers

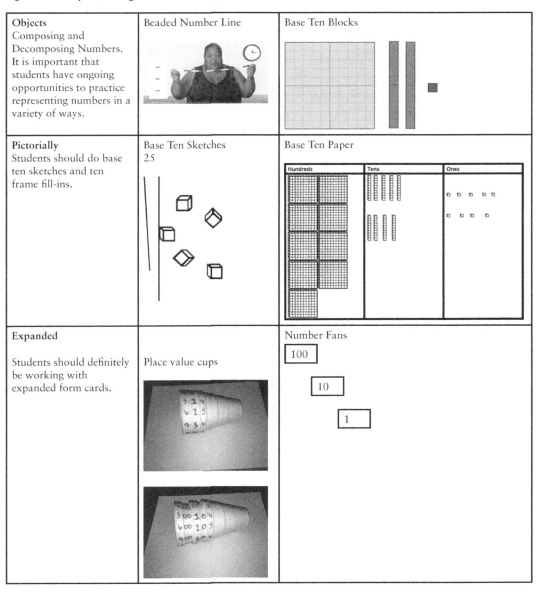

Standard Form	Pull a number card and fill in the table				Pick a number and fill in the diagram
These activities have students working with the standard form along with the other representations.	Word Form	Base Ten Sketch	Standard Form	Expanded Form	Representing Numbers
					Expanded Form / Word Form
					Base Ten Sketch

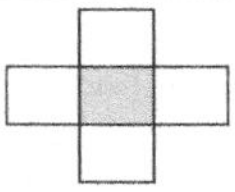

Figure 6.26 More Place Value

Reading Numbers	Writing Numbers
Tic Tac Toe	Pick a card and write that number

Seventeen	Ninety-four	Eighty-three
Forty-one	Fifty-four	Sixty-seven
Seventy-five	Twenty-two	Thirty-nine

Match Games

Ten	Seventy-nine	100
Ten	Fifty-five	One hundred

Fifty

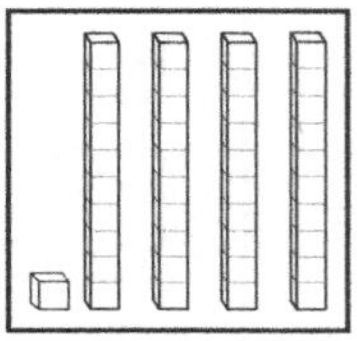

Figure 6.27 Second Grade Workstation

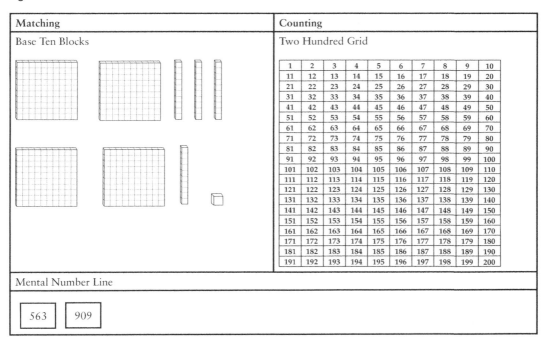

Matching	Counting
Base Ten Blocks	Two Hundred Grid

Mental Number Line
563   909

Figure 6.28 Number Line Activities

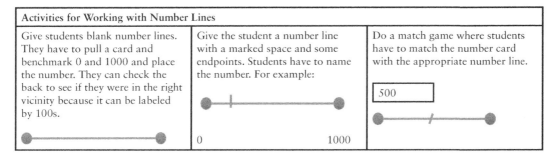

Activities for Working with Number Lines

Give students blank number lines. They have to pull a card and benchmark 0 and 1000 and place the number. They can check the back to see if they were in the right vicinity because it can be labeled by 100s.	Give the student a number line with a marked space and some endpoints. Students have to name the number. For example:	Do a match game where students have to match the number card with the appropriate number line.

State Standards

* Count within 1000; skip-count by 5s, 10s and 100s

(see Figure 6.29).

Figure 6.29 Counting

Abstract
Students should do the other activities mentioned in Chapter 4. In addition they should be doing more abstract work like skip count dot-to-dots and work on the hundred grid. At the abstract level students can shade in the skip count pattern on a hundred grid. I also like to use skip count dot-to-dot pictures because they are self-checking.

1	2	3	4	5	6	7	8	9	10
11	12	13	14	15	16	17	18	19	20
21	22	23	24	25	26	27	28	29	30
31	32	33	34	35	36	37	38	39	40
41	42	43	44	45	46	47	48	49	50
51	52	53	54	55	56	57	58	59	60
61	62	63	64	65	66	67	68	69	70
71	72	73	74	75	76	77	78	79	80
81	82	83	84	85	86	87	88	89	90
91	92	93	94	95	96	97	98	99	100

SECOND GRADE MULTI-DIGIT ADDITION

Second graders are doing a lot of addition. We have to make sure that they are secure in their basic facts. Once they know their basic facts within 20, we need to make sure that they have mastered all of the first grade standards. So in the second grade place value workstation, there should be the first grade place value activities. I guarantee you that not all the second graders have full competency with the first grade standards. The next level is the second grade place value addition and subtraction standards. Students should build the facts, sketch the facts and then work on various strategies to solve the facts.

Start with students working on adding a single digit and a double digit with the beaded number line. Then, have them show this work on the open number line. Continue by having the students add a double digit and a double digit with the beaded number line. After students do this, have them show this work on the open number line. Continue by having students add four two-digit numbers. The goal throughout second grade is to get students to love to play with numbers and not to be afraid of them. We want students to think about different, flexible, efficient ways to add and subtract numbers. We do this through that cycle of engagement of concrete, pictorial and abstract.

After students have mastered adding double digit numbers, then and only then should you work on triple digit numbers. Too often, I go into classrooms where teachers tell me, "well, we're working on three-digit numbers but they don't know how to add two-digit numbers." And I ask, "Why?" They say, "because that is where we are in the pacing calendar." We have got to stop this. This makes NO SENSE. We cannot rush students to three digits when they are still grappling with one and two digits.

Students have to know how to add two-digit numbers before three-digit numbers. I don't feel like I'm going out on a limb saying that! So we have to slow down to speed up! Immediately. The thing is, if we do this correctly, and we actually teach them and let them learn, then when you get to three-digit numbers, or the addition of four two-digit numbers, they know how to do it because they understand conceptually what they are doing (see Figure 6.30). Throughout the year as students work with place value, they need to explain their thinking and discuss their strategies.

Learning Trajectory for Operations in the Second Grade Place Value Centers

Second graders should start by reviewing the first grade place value standard of adding a two-digit number and a one-digit number. They should do this first without regrouping and then with regrouping. They should practice on the number line and on ten frame paper and the hundred grid. Then they continue doing this with two-digit numbers and eventually three-digit numbers. The focus is on using different strategies, such as putting together numbers and taking them apart in different ways (see Figure 6.30). According to Van de Walle, Lovin, Karp, Bay-Williams (2006), students need to be flexible with numbers and able to name them in a variety of ways. Being able to discuss "equivalent representations" is an important part of number sense and helps students with other parts of mathematics.

Figure 6.30 Place Value with Operations

Learning Trajectory for Second Grade Place Value with Operations These stations should stay up all year long as they are taught. There are 12 big topics and within those topics students are working with both operations. This is a lot of learning when laid out like this. Where are your students? Have they mastered everything they need to know in second grade? If they are having trouble, where are they stuck? What can they do and then what do they need to learn next? How will you scaffold it? These are the questions that the idea of leveling workstations address. The philosophy of leveling workstations is that we know exactly where students are so that we can scaffold instruction in such a way that they meet the grade level standards with fluency. Algorithms are "the arithmetic, step-by-step procedures used to find the solution to a computation accurately, reliably and quickly" (Chapin & Johnson, 2006, p. 43).
No Regrouping Addition: two-digit number and one-digit number Subtraction: two-digit number and one-digit number
Regrouping Addition: two-digit number and one-digit number Subtraction: two-digit number and one-digit number
No Regrouping Addition: two-digit number and two-digit number using concrete models or drawings and strategies based on place value, properties of operations and/or the relationship between addition and subtraction relate the strategy to a written method. Subtraction: two-digit number and two-digit number using concrete models or drawings and strategies based on place value, properties of operations and/or the relationship between addition and subtraction relate the strategy to a written method.
Regrouping Addition: two-digit number and two-digit number using concrete models or drawings and strategies based on place value, properties of operations and/or the relationship between addition and subtraction relate the strategy to a written method. Subtraction: two-digit number and two-digit number using concrete models or drawings and strategies based on place value, properties of operations and/or the relationship between addition and subtraction relate the strategy to a written method.
No Regrouping Addition: four two-digit numbers using concrete models or drawings and strategies based on place value, properties of operations and/or the relationship between addition and subtraction relate the strategy to a written method.
Regrouping Addition: four two-digit numbers using concrete models or drawings and strategies based on place value, properties of operations and/or the relationship between addition and subtraction relate the strategy to a written method.
No Regrouping Addition: three-digit number and two-digit number using concrete models or drawings and strategies based on place value, properties of operations and/or the relationship between addition and subtraction relate the strategy to a written method. Subtraction: three-digit number and two-digit number using concrete models or drawings and strategies based on place value, properties of operations and/or the relationship between addition and subtraction relate the strategy to a written method.
Regrouping Addition: three-digit number and three-digit number within 1000 using concrete models or drawings and strategies based on place value, properties of operations and/or the relationship between addition and subtraction. Subtraction: three-digit number and three-digit number within 1000 using concrete models or drawings and strategies based on place value, properties of operations and/or the relationship between addition and subtraction.
Adding 10 to a given number 100–900.
Adding 100 to a given number 100–900.
Subtracting 10 from a given number 100–900.
Subtracting 100 from a given number 100–900.
Explain why addition and subtraction strategies work using place value and the properties of operations.

ADDITION: TWO-DIGIT NUMBER AND ONE-DIGIT NUMBER (FIRST NO REGROUPING/NEXT REGROUPING) (SEE FIGURE 6.31)

Figure 6.31 Adding Two-Digit Numbers

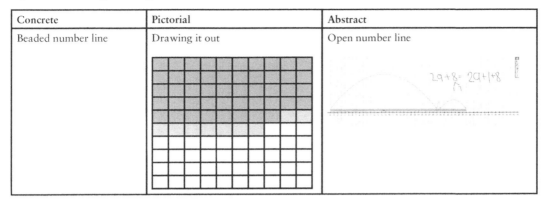

Concrete	Pictorial	Abstract
Beaded number line	Drawing it out	Open number line

SUBTRACTION: TWO-DIGIT NUMBER AND ONE-DIGIT NUMBER (FIRST NO REGROUPING/NEXT REGROUPING) (SEE FIGURE 6.32)

Figure 6.32 Subtracting Two-Digit Numbers

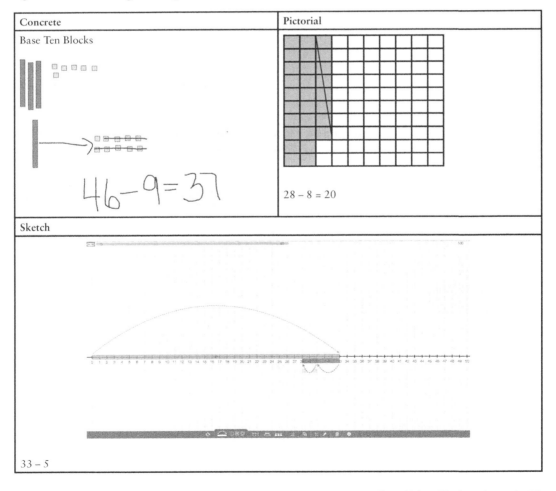

Concrete	Pictorial
Base Ten Blocks	
$46 - 9 = 37$	$28 - 8 = 20$
Sketch	
$33 - 5$	

ADDITION: TWO-DIGIT NUMBER AND TWO-DIGIT NUMBER (FIRST NO REGROUPING/NEXT REGROUPING) (SEE FIGURE 6.33)

Figure 6.33 Adding Two-Digit Numbers

Concrete	Pictorial	Abstract
Beaded Number Line  	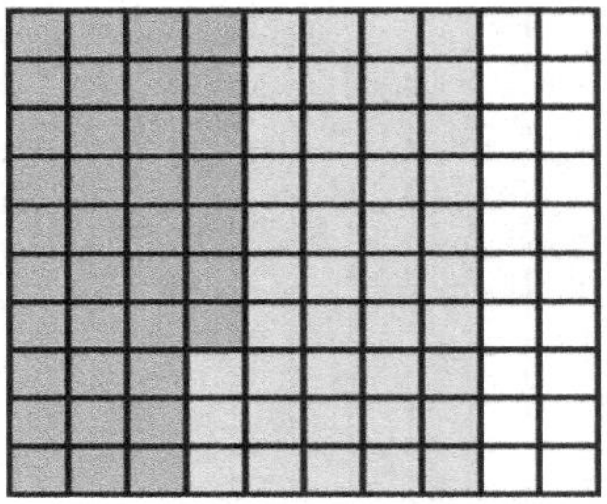	Add 10s then add 1s 37 + 43 30 + 40 = 70 7 + 3 = 10 70 + 10 = 80
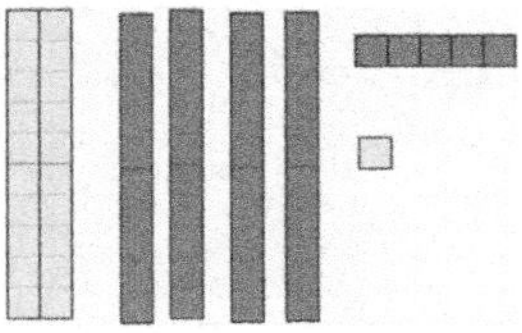	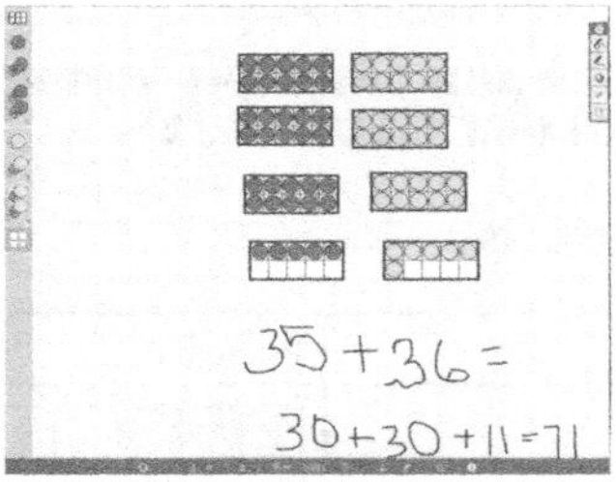 $35 + 36 =$ $30 + 30 + 11 = 71$	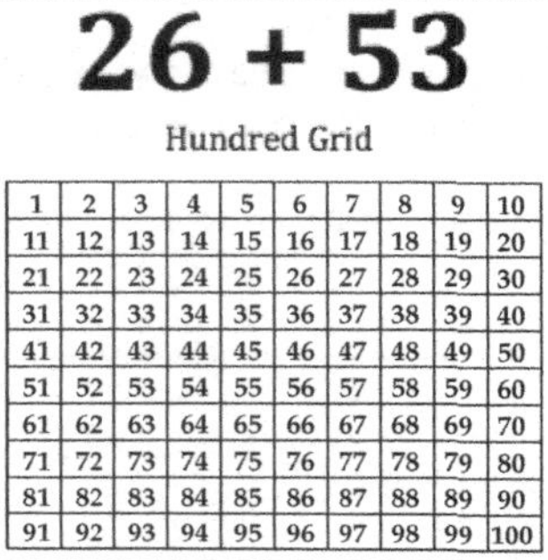 **26 + 53** Hundred Grid

SUBTRACTION: TWO-DIGIT NUMBER AND TWO-DIGIT NUMBER (FIRST NO REGROUPING/NEXT REGROUPING) (SEE FIGURES 6.34 AND 6.35)

Figure 6.34 Subtracting Two-Digit Numbers

Concrete	Pictorial
Beaded Number Line  	37 − 19 = 37 − 20 + 1 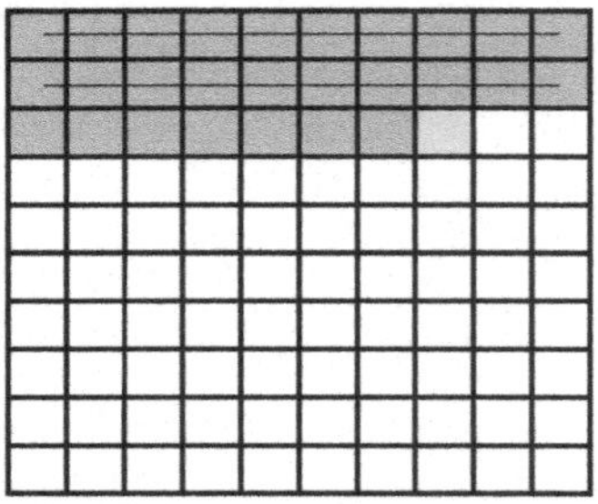

Figure 6.35 Subtracting Two-Digit Numbers

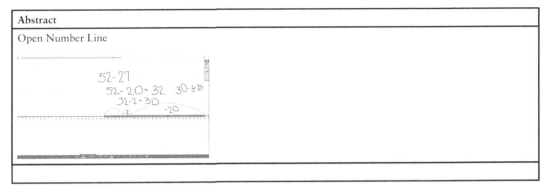

Abstract
Open Number Line

ADDITION: FOUR TWO-DIGIT NUMBERS (FIRST NO REGROUPING/NEXT REGROUPING) (SEE FIGURE 6.36)

Figure 6.36 Adding Two-Digit Numbers

Concrete	Pictorial	Abstract
Students pick build it cards! These cards ask them to build the equation with base ten blocks.  Build it! 20 + 55 + 17 + 25	Students pick sketch it cards. These cards ask them to sketch the equation with base ten blocks. Sketch it! 20 + 55 + 17 + 25	Pick cards where they have to add the numbers and compare with a friend. In terms of adding, students are encouraged to use different strategies. So, maybe they add the 10s and then the 1s. Maybe they use a friendly number strategy. The focus here is not the traditional algorithm but to get students to think strategically. Whoever has the largest sum wins a point. Whoever gets to five points first wins. Add it up! 20 + 55 + 17 + 25 P1　　　P2

ADDITION: THREE-DIGIT NUMBER AND TWO-DIGIT NUMBER (FIRST NO REGROUPING/NEXT REGROUPING) (SEE FIGURE 6.37)

Figure 6.37 Adding Three-Digit Numbers

Concrete	Pictorial	Abstract
Base Ten Blocks	Base Ten Sketch	Open Number Line and Adding from the Left 357 + 25 300 + 50 + 7 20 + 5 300 + 70 + 12 = 382

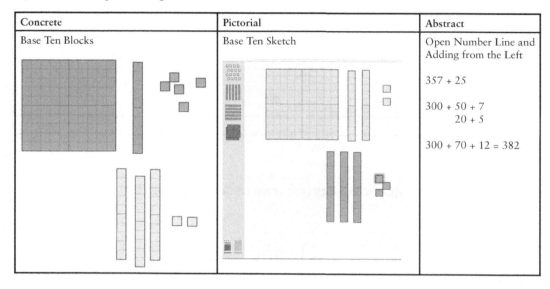

SUBTRACTION: THREE-DIGIT NUMBER AND TWO-DIGIT NUMBER (FIRST NO REGROUPING/NEXT REGROUPING) (SEE FIGURE 6.38)

Figure 6.38 Subtracting Three-Digit Numbers

Concrete	Pictorial	Abstract
Base Ten Blocks 105 – 20 First 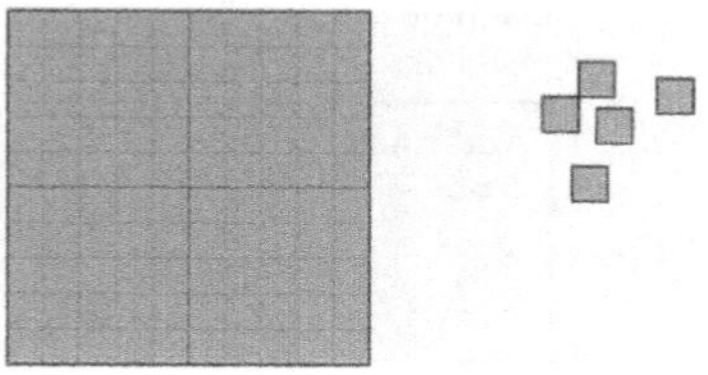 Then 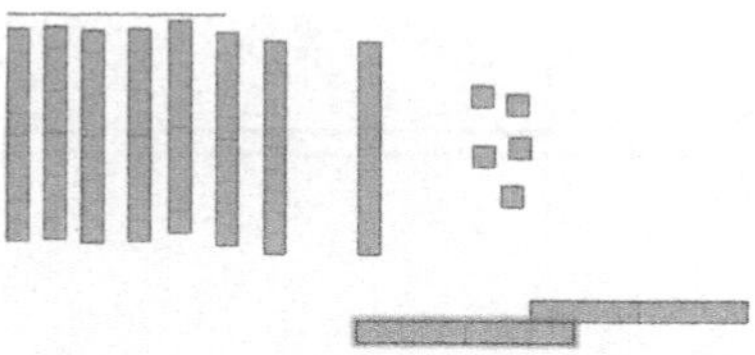	Virtual Base Ten Blocks 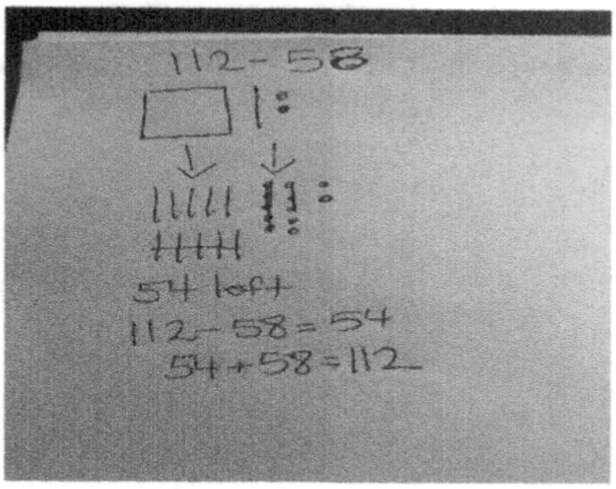 112 – 58 54 left 112 – 58 = 54 54 + 58 = 112	Open Number Line and Adding from the Left 357 – 99 357 + 1 = 358 99 + 1 = 100 358 – 100 = 258

ADDITION: THREE-DIGIT NUMBER AND THREE-DIGIT NUMBER (FIRST NO REGROUPING/NEXT REGROUPING) (SEE FIGURE 6.39)

Figure 6.39 Adding Three-Digit Numbers

Concrete	Pictorial	Abstract
Base Ten Blocks	Virtual Base Ten Blocks	Adding 100s, 10s and 1s Open Number Line
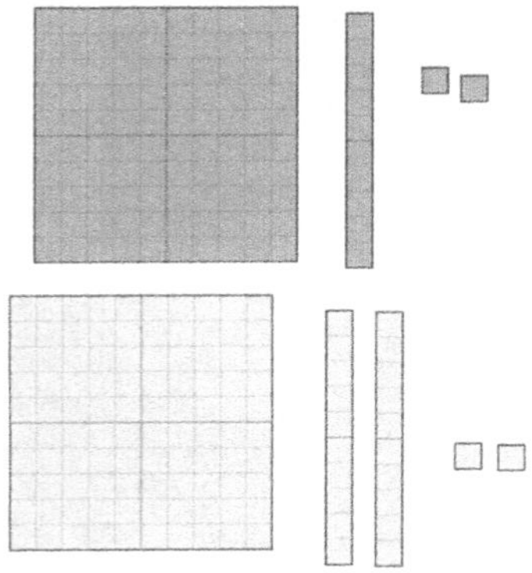	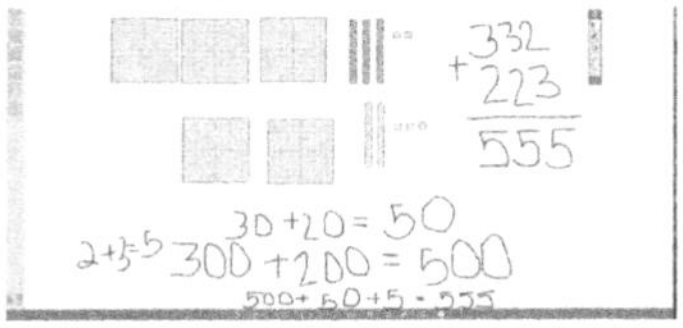	359 + 532 300 + 500 = 800 50 + 30 = 80 9 + 2 = 11 800 + 80 = 880 880 + 11 = 891

SUBTRACTION: THREE-DIGIT NUMBER AND THREE-DIGIT NUMBER (FIRST NO REGROUPING/NEXT REGROUPING) (SEE FIGURE 6.40)

Figure 6.40 Subtracting Three-Digit Numbers

Concrete	Do this with Actual Base Ten Blocks Base Ten Blocks: 300 – 250 First 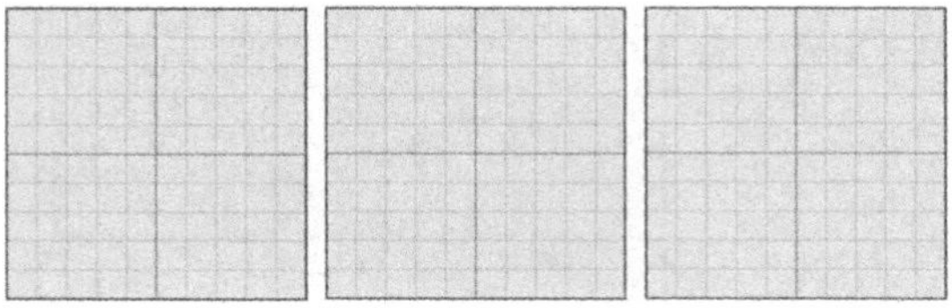 Then 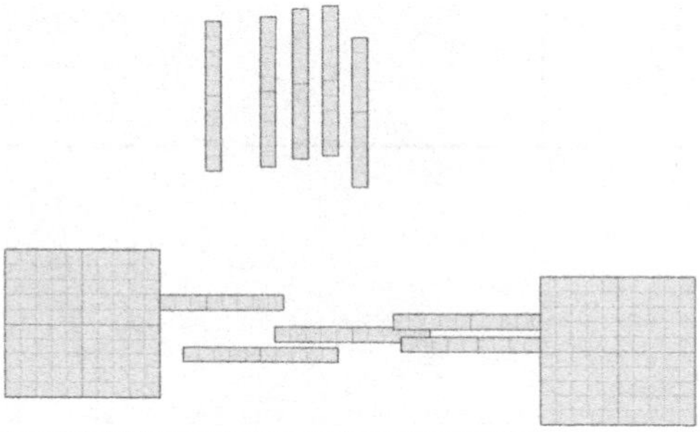
Pictorial	Base Ten Sketch 201 – 30 = 271 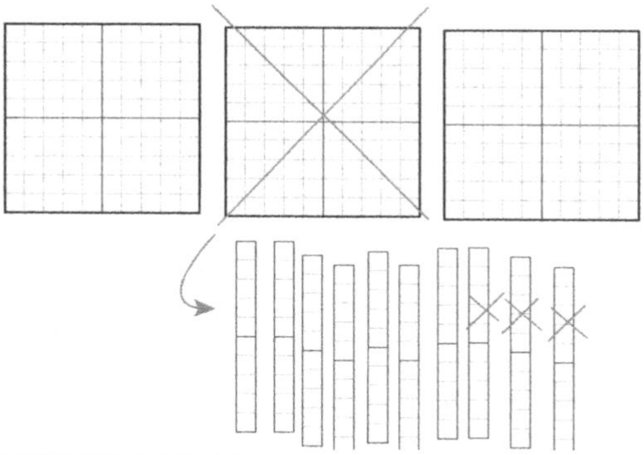
Abstract	Open Number Line and Partial Differences 500 – 311 = 500 – 300 = 200 200 – 11 = 189

Learning to Add and Subtract 10 and 100

Adding and subtracting 10 and 100 from any given number seems easy. Students can do it often-times with the number grid without conceptually understanding what they are doing. It is important that students see and feel the pattern with concrete and virtual manipulatives. I have purpose-fully integrated students working out problems digitally as well as concretely in the examples. We want our students to see the pattern and understand how it works in the base ten system (see Figures 6.41–6.44).

I have detailed workstations that scaffold the understanding of these patterns from the concrete, to the pictorial through the abstract. When planning for and designing workstations it is important that students build a fundamental understanding of the numbers and the patterns connected with those numbers. Yes, eventually, we want students playing board games and card games where they are using these facts, but in the beginning, we must have students working with the pattern so they own that knowledge.

Figure 6.41 Adding 10 to a Given Number 100–900

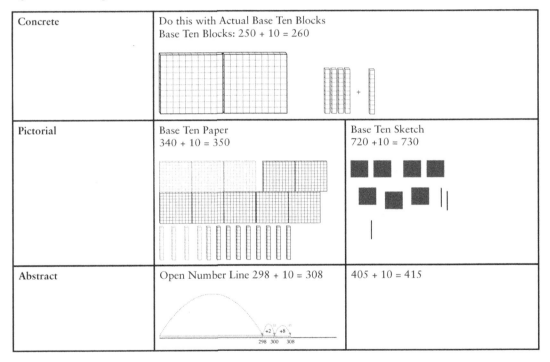

| Concrete | Do this with Actual Base Ten Blocks
Base Ten Blocks: 250 + 10 = 260 | |
| Pictorial | Base Ten Paper
340 + 10 = 350 | Base Ten Sketch
720 +10 = 730 |
| Abstract | Open Number Line 298 + 10 = 308 | 405 + 10 = 415 |

Figure 6.42 Adding 100 to a Given Number 100–900

Concrete	Do this With Actual Base Ten Blocks Base Ten Blocks: 200 + 100 = 300 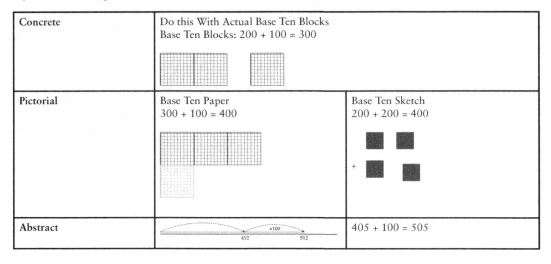	
Pictorial	Base Ten Paper 300 + 100 = 400	Base Ten Sketch 200 + 200 = 400
Abstract	412 +100 512	405 + 100 = 505

Figure 6.43 Subtracting 10 from a Given Number 100–900

Concrete	Base Ten Blocks 600 – 10 = 590	
Pictorial	Base Ten Paper 304 – 10	Base Ten Sketch 330 – 10 = 320
Abstract	Number Grid 190 – 10	Paper and pencil 298 – 10 = 288

Number Grid:

1	2	3	4	5	6	7	8	9	10
11	12	13	14	15	16	17	18	19	20
21	22	23	24	25	26	27	28	29	30
31	32	33	34	35	36	37	38	39	40
41	42	43	44	45	46	47	48	49	50
51	52	53	54	55	56	57	58	59	60
61	62	63	64	65	66	67	68	69	70
71	72	73	74	75	76	77	78	79	80
81	82	83	84	85	86	87	88	89	90
91	92	93	94	95	96	97	98	99	100
101	102	103	104	105	106	107	108	109	110
111	112	113	114	115	116	117	118	119	120
121	122	123	124	125	126	127	128	129	130
131	132	133	134	135	136	137	138	139	140
141	142	143	144	145	146	147	148	149	150
151	152	153	154	155	156	157	158	159	160
161	162	163	164	165	166	167	168	169	170
171	172	173	174	175	176	177	178	179	180
181	182	183	184	185	186	187	188	189	190
191	192	193	194	195	196	197	198	199	200

Figure 6.44 Subtracting 100 from a Given Number 100–900

Concrete	Do this With Actual Base Ten Blocks Base Ten Blocks: 902 – 100 = 802 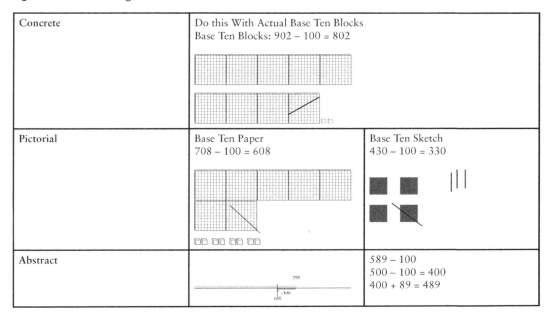	
Pictorial	Base Ten Paper 708 – 100 = 608	Base Ten Sketch 430 – 100 = 330
Abstract		589 – 100 500 – 100 = 400 400 + 89 = 489

Keeping Track of It All

Figure 6.45 Sample Beginning of First Grade Assessment:

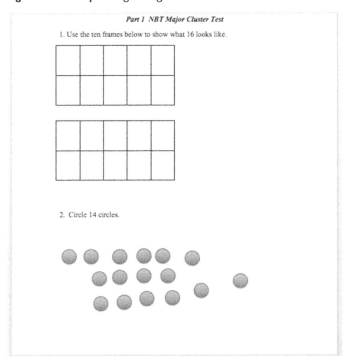

Part 1 NBT Major Cluster Test

1. Use the ten frames below to show what 16 looks like.

2. Circle 14 circles.

Figure 6.45 Continued

3. Draw 17 balls in the box.

4. Circle the picture that shows 15.

5. How many 10s and 1s can you break 12 into?

_____10s   _____1s

6. Write the numbers in the diagram to show how many 10s and how many 1s are in 17?

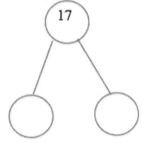

7. Fill in the equation.

10 + _____ = 17

8. Fill in the equation.

8 + _____ = 18

Student Data Example (see Figures 6.46 and 6.47)

Figure 6.46 Place Value Goal: My Place Value Goals

Math	It Looks Like:	Practicing	I Know It!
Add a Two-Digit and a One-Digit Number	37 + 9 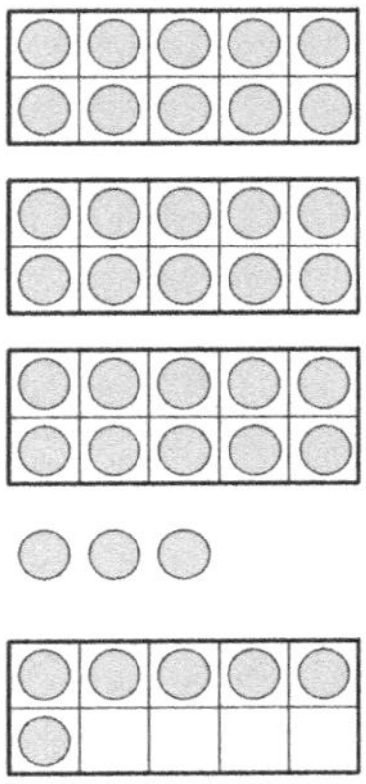		
Subtract 10 From Multiples of 10	50 – 20 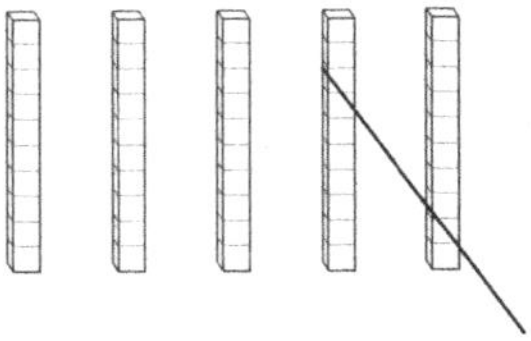		
Add 10 to a Number	46 + 10 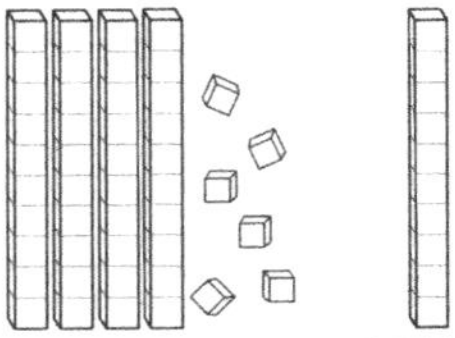		
Compare Numbers with Symbols	Compare the numbers 52 [ ] 37 > | < | =		
Skip Count	2,4,6, 5,10,15		

(Continued)

Figure 6.46 Continued

<table>
<tr><th>Math</th><th>It Looks Like:</th><th>Practicing</th><th>I Know It!</th></tr>
<tr><td>Represent Numbers to 120</td><td>Read and Write
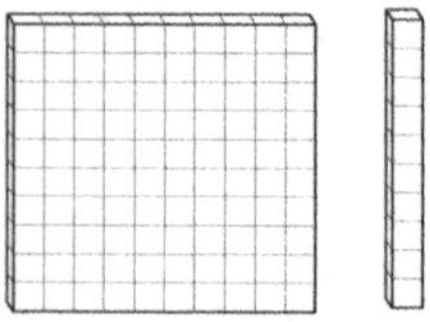
110</td><td></td><td></td></tr>
<tr><td>Count to 120</td><td>
<table>
<tr><td>1</td><td>2</td><td>3</td><td>4</td><td>5</td><td>6</td><td>7</td><td>8</td><td>9</td><td>10</td></tr>
<tr><td>11</td><td>12</td><td>13</td><td>14</td><td>15</td><td>16</td><td>17</td><td>18</td><td>19</td><td>20</td></tr>
<tr><td>21</td><td>22</td><td>23</td><td>24</td><td>25</td><td>26</td><td>27</td><td>28</td><td>29</td><td>30</td></tr>
<tr><td>31</td><td>32</td><td>33</td><td>34</td><td>35</td><td>36</td><td>37</td><td>38</td><td>39</td><td>40</td></tr>
<tr><td>41</td><td>42</td><td>43</td><td>44</td><td>45</td><td>46</td><td>47</td><td>48</td><td>49</td><td>50</td></tr>
<tr><td>51</td><td>52</td><td>53</td><td>54</td><td>55</td><td>56</td><td>57</td><td>58</td><td>59</td><td>60</td></tr>
<tr><td>61</td><td>62</td><td>63</td><td>64</td><td>65</td><td>66</td><td>67</td><td>68</td><td>69</td><td>70</td></tr>
<tr><td>71</td><td>72</td><td>73</td><td>74</td><td>75</td><td>76</td><td>77</td><td>78</td><td>79</td><td>80</td></tr>
<tr><td>81</td><td>82</td><td>83</td><td>84</td><td>85</td><td>86</td><td>87</td><td>88</td><td>89</td><td>90</td></tr>
<tr><td>91</td><td>92</td><td>93</td><td>94</td><td>95</td><td>96</td><td>97</td><td>98</td><td>99</td><td>100</td></tr>
<tr><td>101</td><td>102</td><td>103</td><td>104</td><td>105</td><td>106</td><td>107</td><td>108</td><td>109</td><td>110</td></tr>
<tr><td>111</td><td>112</td><td>113</td><td>114</td><td>115</td><td>116</td><td>117</td><td>118</td><td>119</td><td>120</td></tr>
</table>
</td><td></td><td></td></tr>
</table>

Figure 6.47 Class Snapshot of Adding and Subtracting 10 and 100

	Adding 10 to a Multiple of 10	Subtracting 10 From a Multiple of 10	Subtracting a Multiple of 10 From a Multiple of 10	Subtracting 100	Adding 100
Luke	x				
Tom		x			
Maritza			x		
Kelly			x		
Susie		x			
Joe	x				
Mary		x			
Kiyana		x			
Shakhira	x				
Marcus	x				
Greg			x		
Zeke			x		

Helping Parents/Guardians Help Their Children

Sample Parent/Guardian Letters (see Figures 6.48–6.50)

Figure 6.48 Sample Kindergarten Letter

Dear Parents/Guardians:

We are now studying place value. Here is what we are learning about:

1) Teen number names
2) Breaking apart teen numbers into 10s and 1s
3) Finding teen numbers on the number line
4) Counting teen numbers
5) Representing teen numbers

Tools to Practice:

Number Cards, Rekenrek, Ten Frame and a Number line

We are sending home a rekenrek that we made in school to help practice teen numbers. The top row is our ten and the bottom row is the 1s. Please have your child show you different teen numbers on the rekenrek.

We are also sending home ten frames with mosaics. Please have your child pull a teen card and make that number on the ten frame.

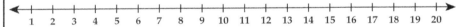

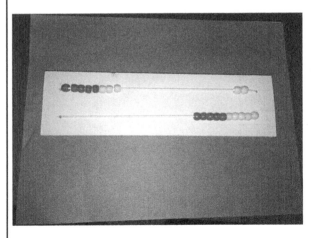

17

11

14

Thank you for helping us teach your child!
Mrs. Carla

Figure 6.49 Sample First Grade Letter

Dear Parents/Guardians,

We are now studying place value. Here is what we are learning about:

1) How to represent two-digit numbers in a variety of ways:
   Meaning 21 could be two 10s and one 1 or 21 1s

2) Finding numbers in the hundred grid:
   Looking for what's before and what's after

3) Counting to 120

Tools to Practice: Number Cards, Rekenrek and Ten Frames
We are sending home a rekenrek that we made in school to help practice making two-digit numbers. Each row has ten beads. Please have your child show you different ways to make two-digit numbers on the rekenrek. There is also a virtual rekenrek. Please see an example below:

We are also sending home ten frames and a crayon. Please have your child pick a two-digit number, practice making two-digit numbers and discuss how many 10s and how many 1s

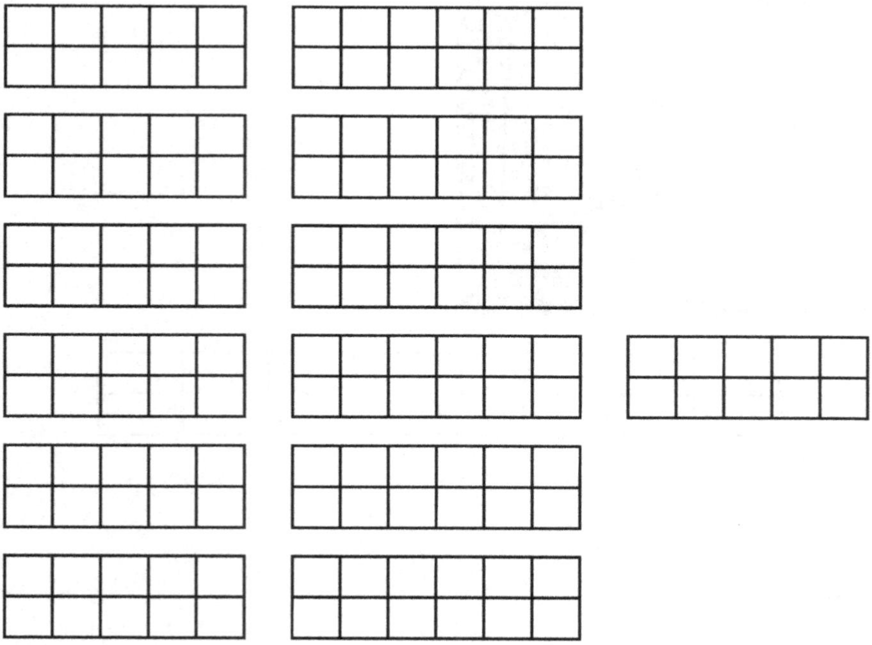

Thank you for helping us teach your child!
Mrs. Carla

Figure 6.50 Sample Second Grade Letter

Dear Parents/Guardians,

We are now studying place value. Here is what we are learning about:

1) How to add two-digit numbers.
2) Our focus right now is how to do it by adding the 10s first and then the 1s. Please use the tools we have sent home to help your child practice.

Tools to Practice: Rekenrek
We are sending home a rekenrek that we made in school to help practice adding two-digit numbers.

For example: 27 + 34 = 20 + 30 + 7 + 4 = 50 + 11 = 61

Here are some problems to practice with your child:

33 + 48

29 + 31

55 + 45

71 + 23

14 + 57

Make up more with a sum no greater than 100.

Thank you for helping us teach your child!
Mrs. Carla

Figure 6.51 Reflection on Workstation Work

1	2	3
Today I didn't work very hard. I did not do what I was supposed to do. Tomorrow I will do better! 	Today I did some of my work. I was off task some of the time. 	I worked really well today. I did all my work. 

Figure 6.52 Getting Started

First: In first and second grade at the beginning of the year, set up the workstations from the year before.
Second: Make sure to do a number of the day routine so that you can review place value throughout the year.
Third: Make sure that you have a variety of tools to teach place value. The tools should be bean sticks, cups and beans as well as bead strings and place value blocks.

Figure 6.53 Research on Place Value in Early Childhood

Researcher	Research	Big Ideas	How does this research inform our practice?
Fuson, K. C. (1990). Conceptual Structures for Multiunit Numbers: Implications for Learning and Teaching Multi-digit Addition, Subtraction, and Place Value. *Cognition and Instruction*, 7(4), 343–403. Tolchinsky, L. (2003). *The Cradle of Culture and What Children Know about Writing and Numbers Before Being Taught.* Mahwah, NJ: Erlbaum.	Place Value Notation.	As many have noted (see Fuson, 1990; Tolchinsky, 2003), place value notation is a "difficult-to-master" system and a complicated one.	Do you work on place value notation throughout the year? In what ways do you work on place value notation in workstations?
Moeller, K., Pixner, S., Zuber, J., Kaufmann, L., & Nuerk, H. C. (2011). Early Place-Value Understanding as a Precursor for Later Arithmetic Performance—A Longitudinal Study on Numerical Development. *Research in Developmental Disabilities*, 32(5), 1837–1851.	Error patterns in place value notation.	"Older children show a characteristic error pattern that goes beyond the mere skipping or inverting of digits in the written string and consists of adding extra digits. That is, when they make mistakes, they typically write the digits in the order in which they heard them, but add extra digits, for example, writing 'six hundred and forty-two' as 600402 or 610042 or 6042, or even sometimes as 61412." "Research shows that students who have trouble with hearing and writing numbers are at risk for difficulties in mathematics" (Moeller et al., 2011).	What error patterns do you notice that your students are doing? What are you doing to correct this? What types of activities might you set up in your workstations to address this error pattern?
Cotter, J. Learning Place Value in First Grade Through Language and Visualization. Activities for Learning, Inc.: Right Start™ Mathematics. Retrieved on June 15, 2018 from Google search: Learning Place Value Research Summary by Joan A. Cotter, Ph.D. (pdf download).	Visualization is very important.	"Visualization vs counting—To understand the importance of visualization, try to see mentally eight apples in a line without any grouping—virtually impossible. Now try to see five of those apples as red and three as green; the vast majority of people can form the mental image" (p. 2).	What types of activities are you using in your workstations to foster students' use of visualization? Do you use place value cards and rekenreks?
Fuson, K. & Briars, D. (1990). Using a Base-Ten Blocks Learning/Teaching Approach for First- and Second-Grade Place-Value and Multidigit Addition and Subtraction. *Journal for Research in Mathematics Education*, 21(3), 180–206.	Place value blocks help to build understanding.	Researchers have found that base ten blocks can be very helpful in teaching children how to add and subtract larger numbers. Research shows that modeling the problems and verbally discussing them helps students to understand the base ten system.	How do you use place value blocks consistently in your place value math workstations?

⚷ Key Points

- Numbers Have a Place and a Value
- There are Many Ways to Represent Numbers
- There are Many Different Strategies to Add and Subtract Numbers

Summary

The development of place value in kindergarten is a foundational domain (see Figure 6.53). Starting in kindergarten students begin to work with the idea of 10s and 1s. This work continues through first grade with a deeper dive into two-digit numbers (see Figure 6.45). In second grade students are expected to know how to work with numbers up to 1000. This takes time and requires distributed practice not only across the year, but also across the grades. Students should do daily activities that are reinforced in the math workstations throughout the year (see Figures 6.51 and 6.52).

Reflection Questions

1. Is place value something that you teach all year? What stands out for you in this chapter?
2. How is this chapter going to inform your teaching and learning environment?
3. How will this chapter help you to structure the types of support you can give the parents/guardians to help their children throughout the year?

References

Fuson, K. & Briars, D. (1990). Using a Base-Ten Blocks Learning/Teaching Approach for First- and Second-Grade Place-Value and Multidigit Addition and Subtraction. *Journal for Research in Mathematics Education*, 21(3), 180–206. doi:10.2307/749373.

National Governors Association Center for Best Practices and the Council of Chief State School Officers. (2010). *Common Core State Standards for Mathematics*. Retrieved on June 15, 2018 http://www.corestandards.org/Math/Practice.

Van de Walle, J., Lovin, L., Karp, K., & Bay-Williams, J. (2018/2006). *Students-Centered Mathematics*. NY: Pearson.

7

Fluency Workstations

Surely not everybody needs to practice the "Make Ten Game"?

Dolch Words of Math

When I look in the fluency station, I see traditional flashcards, some dominos and some make ten games. I stop and wonder, "Is everybody working on make ten, still (it's February)?" Probably not. Surely, somebody is working on doubles or bridging ten. This common scenario is the very reason why we need leveled workstations. Fluency strategies are along a continuum and as students learn them, they need to practice the next steps (see Figure 7.1). Baroody (2006) calls it the Phases of Mastery. Battista (2012) calls it the Levels of Sophistication. I call it "The Dolch Words of Math." That's because I used to be a literacy person, and in literacy there are Dolch words that you learn so that you can read fluently. The same idea applies in math. There are certain things we need to know (like the basic facts) so we can do the other stuff in math. This continuum has been discussed by many researchers. Basic facts for addition and subtraction are sums and differences within 20. Students should learn their facts rather than memorize them. If you just memorize them, then you can easily forget them. If you learn them, then you can always do them through a variety of strategies, based in place value, properties and the relationships between the operations (NCTM, 2000; National Governors Association, 2010; Henry & Brown, 2008).

Strategy Talk

As students are learning their facts, there are different approaches to working with numbers. These strategies have names (see Figure 7.2).

Fluency as a Four-Legged Stool

Fluency is a multi-dimensional concept. We can think of it as a four-legged stool: accuracy, flexibility, efficiency and instant recall. The stool only stands with all four legs, and if it only has the instant recall leg, it will fall. When students have all four, they have full fluency. The way they get full fluency is to work with number combinations in a variety of engaging, interactive, rigorous, student-friendly activities that build a foundational understanding of how numbers are in relationship with each other. The research resoundingly states that computational fluency is multi-dimensional (speed and accuracy, flexibility and efficiency) (Brownell, 1935; Brownell, 1956/1987; Kilpatrick, Swafford, & Findell, 2001; National Council of Teachers of Mathematics, 2000).

Figure 7.1 Fluency

Big Ideas There is a learning continuum for basic facts. There are different types of strategy levels on a continuum from unsophisticated (counting on fingers) to sophisticated (using derived facts and learned facts).	Enduring Understandings There are many strategies to add and subtract numbers. There are many ways to model thinking.
Essential Questions What are addition strategies and how do they help us to learn our basic facts? What are subtraction strategies and how do they help us to learn our basic facts?	Know/Do Add and subtract using flexible and efficient strategies.

Figure 7.2 Strategies

5 + 7				
Counted All	**Counted On**	**Known Facts**	**Derived Facts**	**Automatic Facts**
Students count out the first addend, then they count out the second addend, then they count the total. 5 + 7 Sounds like: 1, 2, 3, 4, 5 then 1, 2, 3, 4, 5, 6, 7 then 1, 2, 3, 4, 5, 6, 7, 8, 9, 10, 11, 12	There are different types of counting on. . . . One is when students start at whatever addend comes first; the next level is when students consistently start with the higher addend. 5 + 7 Sounds like: 7 – 8, 9, 10, 11, 12	These are facts that students just know . . . often times they are intermittent, with really no rhyme or reason . . . they could be random facts. But they could be things like doubles . . . many students know that 5 + 5 is 10 without thinking about it.	These are facts where students use what they know to figure out new facts. So here they might say well 5 + 5 is 10 and 2 more is 12.	This is when students know their facts without having to think about them. Logan (1991a) calls this the "instant popping into of mind."

Fluency is a four-legged stool

If one of the legs is missing—then students only have partial fluency. Students can know all their facts instantly and not have any number sense.

The Four Legs of Fluency are: Accuracy, Flexibility, Efficiency and Automaticity

Cycle of Engagement: Concrete, Representational, Abstract

Students should work on number combination activities through a cycle of concrete, pictorial and abstract. Working in various ways with facts deepens understanding (Anstrom, 2017; Bender, 2009; Devlin, 2000; Van de Walle, 2001; Maccini & Gagnon, 2000). Leveling workstations addresses the idea that meaningful practice should be individualized (Van de Walle, 2007) (see Figure 7.3). When students are working in their zone of proximal development (Vygotsky, 1978), then they are not bored or frustrated. They can actually build a solid foundation of understanding. This specifically looks like some students working on making ten facts and other students working on making doubles. Everyone is working toward the grade level standard but at their own pace.

How Does All This Work?

Assess

The teacher assesses the student with a Math Running Record or a Fluency Probe (see Figures 7.4 and 7.5). Math Running Records is a way to assess all of the aspects of fluency and then provide the information for what should be done next (Newton, 2016). There has been much research done on specific facts and the ways in which students solve these facts (Isaacs & Carroll, 1999; Van de Walle, 2004; Sherin & Fuson, 2005). The benchmark problems used in the Math Running Records draw upon this prior research.

There is also another type of assessment called a two-color probe. There are two parts to this test. In Part A the teacher gives the students two different colors. The students start the test in one color and then switch to another color after a minute or so (depending on how many problems are on the test). In Part B the students are asked questions about fluency, efficiency and accuracy. This type of assessment can give you so much quick information and yet it doesn't stress students out like many timed tests do. The teacher gets to see who was able to do it in the first color (they have automaticity), who was able to finish all correct in the second color (they have accuracy) and who couldn't do it at all or who did it all and got them all wrong. It provides a wealth of information.

Figure 7.3 Cycle of Assessment

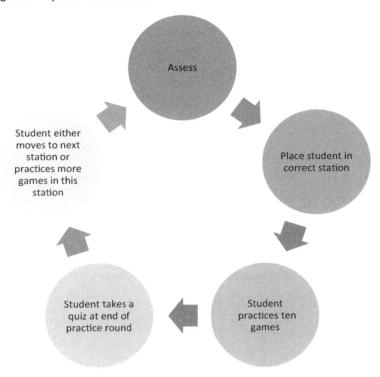

Figure 7.4 Addition Running Record

Addition Running Record Recording Sheet		
Part 1	Codes (What do you notice?)	
0 + 1 a 5s pth	fca fco cah coh dk ic wo sc asc	A0—add 0
2 + 1 a 5s pth	fca fco cah coh dk ic wo sc asc	A1—add 1
3 + 2 a 5s pth	fca fco cah coh dk ic wo sc asc	Aw5—add w/in 5
2 + 6 a 5s pth	fca fco cah coh dk ic wo sc asc	Aw10—add w/in 10
4 + 6 a 5s pth	fca fco cah coh dk ic wo sc asc	AM10– add making 10
10 + 4 a 5s pth	fca fco cah coh dk ic wo sc asc	A10 add 10 to a #
7 + 7 a 5s pth	fca fco cah coh dk ic wo sc asc	AD—add doubles
5 + 6 a 5s pth	fca fco cah coh dk ic wo sc asc	AD1 –add dbls +/- 1
7 + 5 a 5s pth	fca fco cah coh dk ic wo sc asc	AD2—add dbls +/- 2
9 + 6 a 5s pth	fca fco cah coh dk ic wo sc asc	AHF/C9 add higher facts/use compensation w/9
8 + 4 a 5s pth	fca fco cah coh dk ic wo sc asc	AHF/C 7/8 add higher facts/ use compensation with 7/8
7 + 8 a 5s pth	fca fco cah coh dk ic wo sc asc	AHF/C7/8 add higher facts/use compensation with 7/8

Codes:

a– automatic
5s - 5 seconds
pth - prolonged thinking time

fca—finger counted all
fco—finger counted on
cah - counted all in head
coh—counted on in head
dk - didn't know
ic—in context (could tell when set in a story)

wo—wrong operation
sc– self-corrected
asc - attempted to self-correct

General Observations (to be filled out after interview)

   *In most states 1st grade has an expectation of fluency within 10.

Instructional Response:

Focus areas (circle all that apply): flexibility   accuracy   automaticity
Strategy to begin instruction: A0   A1   Aw5   Aw10 AM10 A10   AD   AD1   AD2   AHF/9   AHF/7/8
Strategy level for current strategy: 0 1 2 3 4M 4 _____
(if student was counting on, describe the process: fca or fco 1st addend, larger addend or if student counted on in head ask and note cah or coh 1st addend or larger addend)

Figure 7.4 Continued

Part 2	Add 1 2 + 1	Add w/in 5 or 10 3 + 2 2 + 6	Add Make Ten 4 + 6	Add 10 10 + 4
Add 0 0 + 1 What happens when you are adding zero to a number? ___same # ___can't articulate 8 + 0 5 + 0	What happens when you are adding one to a number? ___ next counting # ___ can't articulate 4 + 1 10 + 1	If your friend didn't know how to solve these problems, what would you tell them to do? ___ count on from big# ___ can't articulate w/in5 w/in10 1 + 4 | 3 + 4 2 + 3 | 2 + 7	What is 8 + 2? What is 3 + 7 I'm going to give you a number and I want you to give me the number that makes 10 with it. If I give you 5, how many more to make 10? 9? 6? 2? 4? 3?	What is happening when we add 10 to a number? ___ teen #'s decompose to 10 and 1's ___ can't articulate 10 + 2 10 + 8
Do they know this strategy? No/Emerging/Yes A0 Level: 0 1 2 3 4M 4	Do they know this strategy? No/Emerging/Yes A1 Level: 0 1 2 3 4M 4	Do they know this strategy? No/Emerging/Yes Aw10 Lvl: 0 1 2 3 4M 4	Do they know this strategy? No/Emerging/Yes AM10 Lvl: 0 1 2 3 4M 4	Do they know this strategy? No/Emerging/Yes A10 Lvl: 0 1 2 3 4M 4
Doubles 7 + 7 What is 8 + 8? ___ 6 + 6? _____ 9 + 9? _____ What kinds of facts are these? _____	Dbls +/-1 5 + 6 How did you figure out 5 + 6? ___ Dbls +/- 1 ___ other ___ can't articulate What is 6 + 7? ___ Dbls +/- 1 ___ other ___ can't articulate	Dbls +/-2 7 + 5 If a friend did not know how to solve this problem, what would you tell them to do? ___ Dbls +/- 2 ___ other ___ can't articulate Could you figure out 6 + 8 for me? ___ Dbls +/- 2 ___ other ___ can't articulate	Bridge through 10 (9) 9 + 6 What strategy did you use to solve this problem? ___ Bridge 10 ___ other ___ can't articulate How would you figure out 9 + 4? ___ Bridge 10 ___ other ___ can't articulate	Bridge through 10 (7/8) 8 + 4 7 + 8 What strategy did you use to solve these problems? ___ Bridge 10 ___ other ___ can't articulate How would you solve 8 + 5? ___ Bridge 10 ___ other ___ can't articulate
Do they know this strategy? No/Emerging/Yes AD Level: 0 1 2 3 4M 4	Do they know this strategy? No/Emerging/Yes AD1 Lvll: 0 1 2 3 4M 4	Do they know this strategy? No/Emerging/Yes AD2 Lvll: 0 1 2 3 4M 4	Do they know this strategy? No/Emerging/Yes AHF/C 9 Level: 0 1 2 3 4M 4	Do they know this strategy? No/Emerging/Yes AHF/C 7/8 Level: 0 1 2 3 4M 4

Part 3

Do you like math?

What did you find easy?

What did you find tricky?

What do you do when you get stuck?

Codes:
0 - doesn't know
1 - counting strategies fingers or manipulatives
2 - mental math/solve in head
3 - derived facts
4M - automatic recall memorized
4 - automatic recall with understanding
fca—finger counted all
fco—finger counted on
cah - counted all in head
coh—counted on in head
ic - in context
dk - didn't know

Note: See updated MRR at this link: https://mathrunningrecords.wordpress.com/.

Figure 7.5 Two-Colored Fluency Probe

Solve:

A.	B.	C.
1 + 9 =	2 + 0 =	4 + 7 =
D.	E.	F.
5 + 5 =	3 + 8 =	12 + 8 =
G.	H.	I.
8 + 7 =	5 + 7 =	9 + 9 =
J.	The End	
5 + 9 =		

A.	B.	C.
10 – 4 =	18 – 9 =	12 – 11 =
D.	E.	F.
8 – 6 =	14 – 14 =	20 – 9 =
G.	H.	I.
17 – 7 =	15 – 10 =	7 – 1 =
J.	The End	
8 – 0 =		

1. If a friend were stuck adding 7 + 9, what would you tell them to do?

2. What is another way to solve 5 + 9 = ?
   a. 5 + 9 + 9 = ?
   b. 9 – 5 = ?
   c. 10 + 4 = ?
   d. None of the above

3. Which addition fact can help you solve 9 – 5 = ?
   a. 9 + 5 = 14
   b. 5 + 4 = 9
   c. 9 + 14 = 23
   d. None of the above
4. Maribel said that 5 + 6 is 12. Is she correct? Explain how you know.

Place Student in Correct Level

The teacher uses the data to decide which level of workstation to place the student. This is based on how the student did on the assessment. Students will start at different levels. This is just like determining which level reader they should start with (see Figure 7.6). Students will progress through these levels at different rates.

Figure 7.6 Strategies

Addition	Subtraction
Plus 1	Minus 1
Plus 0	Minus 0
Count On 1, 2, 3	Take a number away from itself
Add within 5	Count Back 1, 2, 3
Make 5	Subtract within 5
Add within 10	Subtract from 5
Make 10	Subtract within 10
Add 10	Subtract from 10
Doubles	Subtract 10 from a teen number
Doubles Plus 1	Subtract 1s from a teen number
Doubles Plus 2	Subtracting differences of 1 or 2
Adding 7, 8, 9	Subtract by bridging 10
Adding within 20	Fact Families
Make 20	Subtract from 20

Concrete, Pictorial and Abstract Activities

They should do at least three activities each from the concrete, pictorial and abstract columns. Sometimes the activities stand on their own. Other times, the activities all work together. For example, students might be playing a flashcard doubles rekenrek game. They first would build the activity on the rekenrek, next they would draw the fact on the rekenrek and finally they would write the equation with the answer. This could all take place at the same time. This cycle actually helps students to connect the three (see Figures 7.7 and 7.8).

Figure 7.7 Workstation Checklist Example

Make Ten Workstation Checklist		
Concrete Activities Pick 3	Pictorial Activities Pick 3	Abstract Activities Pick 3
Flashcard Build It!	Picture Flashcards/Ten Frame Flashcards	Make Ten Card Game 1
Shake and Show!	Ten Frame Spin to 10	Make Ten Card Game 2
Number Bracelet to Ten	Number Bracelet Draw and Show	Make Ten Flashcards (Number Bracelet)
Rekenrek Build and Show	Rekenrek Build and Show	Make Ten Flashcards Just Numbers
"Ten Stick" Build & Draw	"Ten Stick" Build & Draw	Make Ten Tic-Tac-Toe
Adding Machine/Part-Part Whole Mats		Spin to Ten

Figure 7.8 A Rekenrek Example

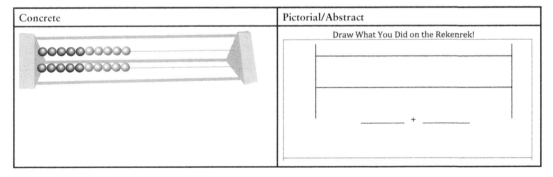

Concrete	Pictorial/Abstract
	Draw What You Did on the Rekenrek!

Student Practices Ten Games

Students need and want choice. It is important to give the student a variety of activities and games to choose from (see Figures 7.9 and 7.10). There should be a mix of alone games, partner games and small group games. Many of these same games you will use in your guided math groups with questioning. You might also send some of these same games home for students to play with their parents or guardians.

Here is a subtraction example:

Figure 7.9 Subtraction Workstation Example

Take From Ten Workstation Checklist		
Concrete Activities Pick 3	Pictorial Activities Pick 3	Abstract Activities Pick 3
Flashcard Build It!	Picture Flashcards	Game Board 1: Superhero Subtraction
Ten Frame Take Away!	Ten Frame Flashcards	Game Board 2: Superhero Spinner
Number Bracelet Take from Ten	Number Bracelet Draw and Show	Popsicle Stick Facts
Rekenrek Take from Ten	Rekenrek Build and Show	Roll and Find the Difference
"Ten Sticks" Build & Break & Show	"Ten Sticks" Build & Break & Show	Fact Family Fun! Hexagon Flashcards
Subtraction Machine/Part-Part Whole Mats	Roll and Draw A Take From Ten Fact	Subtract Ten Tic-Tac-Toe

Figure 7.10 More Examples of Concrete, Pictorial and Abstract Activities

Concrete/Pictorial/Abstract		
Students build a ten tower with cubes. Then, they roll the dice and subtract that many cubes.	Students then record their activity on the recording sheet. Then they write the equation.	Students then record the equation.

Act out a problem with cubes.

Step 1: Build it with cubes.
Step 2: Color it in.
Step 3: Break off the cubes the problem shows.
Step 4: Cross those cubes off on your template.

7–5

Sometimes students just work on an activity that focuses on concrete, pictorial or abstract. For example, students might play a board game or flashcards and they are working on instant recall and not using any concrete materials or visual manipulatives (see Figure 7.11).

Figure 7.11 Abstract Activities

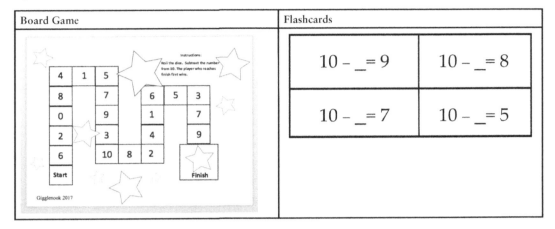

Assess Again

After students have had an opportunity to practice the strategy in a variety of ways and they think they are ready, they can take a quiz and be interviewed by the teacher. The quiz is going to give you some insight into what the student knows, but the oral mini-interview around the strategy is going to fill out the information (see Figures 7.12 and 7.13).

Figure 7.12 Example of an Addition Assessment

Make Ten Quiz	
Match Numbers that Make Ten 5 3 9 8 7 6 4 5 2 1	Fill in the numbers: 5 + _____ = 10 _____ + 3 = 10 4 + _____ = 10 _____ + 10 = 10 1 + _____ = 10

	Circle all the expressions that make ten	
_____ + _____ = 10 10 = _____ + _____	4 + 4	5 + 5
	7 + 3	9 + 0
	1 + 6	8 + 2
	5 + 4	6 + 3

Figure 7.13 Example of a Subtraction Assessement

Take From Ten Quiz	
1. Write and Model a Fact on the Ten Frame. A. _[ten frame grid]_ 10 – _____ = _____ B. _[ten frame grid]_ 10 – _____ = _____	2. Fill in the numbers: A. 10 – _____ = 6 B. 10 – 5 = _____ C. _____ – 0 = 10 D. 10 – _____ = 1 E. 10 – 2 = _____
3. Solve. Model your thinking with a drawing. A. 10 – 5 = _____ B. 10 – 10 = _____	4. Fill in the boxes. _[box with 10 on top, 6 bottom left]_ _[box with 10 on top, 9 bottom right]_

Teacher Mini-Interview

So Kelly, you have been practicing your Take From Ten facts.

- What are Take From Ten facts?
- Why are they important?
- What strategies do you use when you are solving them?
- If you saw 10–5, what would you do? How would you solve it? What would you think?

Next Steps

After students have taken the quiz and done the mini-interview with the teacher, the teacher needs to decide what comes next. The student might need to practice some more of the particular facts that they were working on, or they might be ready to go to the next level. The teacher tells the student what is going to happen next and why.

A Note About Games

*Games and the activities that the students do are a variety of specific structures. When students go to the stations, they should know how to play the game. They are working on a different strategy but they know how to play the cup game, how to sort dominos or how to do clip cards.

Helping Parents/Guardians Help Their Children

(The importance of laying out the landscape)

Here is a framework for parent fluency involvement:

- Letter
- Game Boards
- Flashcards
- Online Games (when possible)

(see Figures 7.14–7.20)

Parents need to know the 4 legs of fluency. This is best explained in a letter and a video link. In this letter you want to discuss the importance of accuracy, flexibility, efficiency and eventually automaticity.

The depth of the letter depends on the parent population that you work with. Although parents should know the continuums, sometimes when you give them the whole continuum, they try to rush their children through instead of taking it at a slower pace.

Figure 7.14 Parent/Guardian Communication

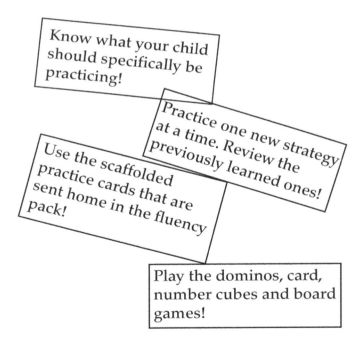

How can I help my child with math?

Know what your child should specifically be practicing!

Practice one new strategy at a time. Review the previously learned ones!

Use the scaffolded practice cards that are sent home in the fluency pack!

Play the dominos, card, number cubes and board games!

Figure 7.15 Parent and Guardian Communication

Math Facts Homework

Dear Families,

We are studying our basic math facts. Research shows that learning math facts includes four things: accuracy, flexibility, efficiency and automaticity.

Accuracy: We want all of our students to know the correct answer. They LEARN the facts by practicing them through a variety of activities.

Flexibility: We will be playing several games to build flexibility. We want students to have number sense. We want them to think about and be flexible with numbers. This means that we will work on our facts through strategies rather than sheer memorization.

Efficiency: Efficiency means that students can pick quick ways to arrive at the answers based on the numbers that they are using.

Automaticity: Instant recall. Learned facts.

Figure 7.16 Parent and Guardian Communication

Your child will be working through a ladder of facts. Here is the sequence:

- Level 1 – Plus 1
- Level 2 – Plus 0
- Level 3 – Plus 2
- Level 4 – Count on facts
- Level 5 – Add within 5
- Level 6 – Make 5
- Level 7 – Adding within 10
- Level 8 – Making 10
- Level 9 – Add 10
- Level 10 – Doubles
- Level 11 – Doubles Plus 2
- Level 12 – Double Plus 2
- Level 13 – Bridge 7
- Level 14 – Bridge 8
- Level 15 – Bridge 9
- Level 16 – Adding Higher Facts 11, 12, 13, 14, 15
- Level 17 – Adding Higher Facts 16, 17, 18, 19
- Level 18 – Make 20 facts
- Level 19 – Adding Facts within 20
- Level 20 – General Review

Your child is working on Level —————. In this packet you will find a variety of concept cards and games to work on with your child. Your child will also have a Ring of Facts. On this ring are all the facts they know, plus the new set.

Thank you for your help at home!

Figure 7.17 Parent and Guardian Communication

Dear Parent/Guardian:

Your child is working on half facts. In this pack you will find two things to practice:

1)   Half Fact Flashcards
2)   A Half Fact Game board

The flashcards:

2 – 1	4 – 2	6 – 3	8 – 4	10 – 5
12 – 6	14 – 7	16 – 8	18 – 9	20 – 10

Figure 7.18 The Gameboard:

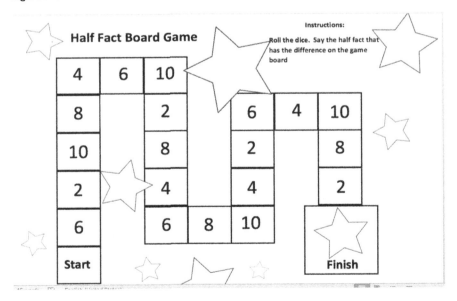

Figure 7.19 Goal Setting

		Goal	Examples	Practicing	Fluent
		Doubles Facts 	8 + 8 7 + 7 4 + 4		
		Doubles + 1 Facts 	5 + 6 4 + 5 7 + 8		
 BAM!!		Doubles + 2 Facts 	8 + 6 7 + 9 5 + 7		
		Add + 10 	10 + 9 10 + 2 5 + 10		
 BAM!!		Adding 7, 8, or 9 	8 + 5 9 + 6 5 + 7		

Figure 7.20 Class Snapshot

	Adding Zero	Counting On	Adding Within 10	Adding 10	Make 10	Doubles	Doubles +1	Doubles +2	Bridging 10	Adding Higher Numbers
Luke										
Tom										
Maritza										
Kelly										
Susie										
Joe										
Mary										
Kiyana										
Shakhira										
Marcus										
Greg										
Zeke										

Figure 7.21 Getting Started

1. Find resources that teach the strategies. Look at my pinterest math strategy board for class anchor chart ideas: www.pinterest.com/drnicki7/math-strategies/
2. Look at the **Math Learning Center Addition and Subtraction Strategy** posters.
3. Look at Mr. Elementary's Strategy Resources.
4. Look at Sara Master's Strategy Flashcards: www.guided-math-adventures.com/?page_id=124
5. Look at the Pimser Printable Fluency Resources: https://kentuckymathematics.org/pimser_printables.php

Figure 7.22 Research on Learning Math

Researcher	Research	Big Ideas	How Does This Research Inform Our Practice?
Pape and Tchoshanov (2001)	Representations are important and how we represent problems impacts students' thinking and how they are thinking impacts how they represent problems. We have to work on developing our teaching around representation.	They discuss how representation is "a two-sided process, an interaction of internalization of external representations and externalization of mental images" (p. 119). We need to get our students to visualize more and then discuss and express those visualizations.	How do you integrate representation throughout the activities that students do in math workstations?
Ball and Bass (2003)	Students need to know how to represent their thinking.	Representation is very important. Teachers need to know how to represent ideas and procedures to students.	
Lesh et al. (1987)	There are five different types of representations.	Lesh et al. (1987) note that there are five different types of representations: • manipulative models • real scripts • static pictures • written symbols • spoken language	How do you weave the five different types of representations throughout the practice activities in the math workstations?
Lesh et al. (1987)	Students should be able to go back and forth between the five different types of representations.	Lesh et al. (1987) argue that students should not only know the five different types of representations but should be able to make connections between them.	Do your workstation activities give students opportunities to work with concepts in a variety of ways?
Janvier (1987)	Understanding is built through developing activities where students can look at, discuss and explain different representations.	"Understanding is a cumulative process mainly based upon the capacity of dealing with an ever-enriching set of representations." (p. 67).	In thinking about scaffolding understanding, how do you design workstation activities so that students are working with "an ever-enriching set of representations"?

⚷ Key Points

- Research-Based Trajectories
- Concrete, Pictorial, Abstract
- Leveled Workstations
- Ten Activities
- Quiz
- Teacher Mini-Interview

Summary

Leveled Math Workstations give students the opportunity to engage in meaningful practice at their instructional level. They are based on the research-based learning continuums for addition and subtraction. There are different types of assessments that can help us to determine where students are on the learning continuum. After we assess, we give students a variety of activities to practice where they are on the continuum and then we reassess them. If they have learned the strategies we move them on to the next level, but if they are still struggling, we have them practice some more. Students move at their own pace throughout the year, all the while being exposed to the taught/bought curriculum but being allowed to practice in their "zone of proximal development" (Vygotsky, 1978). If we give students a chance to understand the number combinations and practice them until they "own them," then they will have a profound sense of number that sets them up to do well with more advanced math skills (see Figures 7.21 and 7.22).

Reflection Questions

1. In what ways are you currently framing your fluency work around the "Dolch words of math"?
2. In what ways are you teaching the facts through a concrete, pictorial and then abstract cycle?
3. How are you scaffolding learning the facts so that parents and guardians can help in a meaningful way?

References

Anstrom, T. (n.d.). *Supporting Students in Mathematics Through the Use of Manipulatives.* Washington, DC: Center for Implementing Technology in Education. November 15, 2017.

Ball, D. L. & Bass, H. (2003). Toward a Practice-Based Theory of Mathematical Knowledge for Teaching. In B. Davis & E. Simmt (Eds.), Proceedings of the 2002 Annual Meeting of the Canadian Mathematics Education Study Group. Edmonton, AB: CMESG/GCEDM, pp. 3–14.

Baroody, A. J. (2006). Why Children Have Difficulties Mastering the Basic Number Combinations and How to Help Them. *Teaching Children Mathematics,* 13, 22–32.

Battista, M. (2012). *Cognition-Based Assessment & Teaching of Addition and Subtraction.* Portsmouth, NH: Heinemann.

Bender, W. (2009). *Differentiating Math Instruction: Strategies That Work for K-* Classroom.* Thousand Oaks: Corwin Press.

Brownell, W. A. (1935). Psychological Considerations in the Learning and the Teaching of Arithmetic. In W. D. Reeve (Ed.), *The Teaching of Arithmetic (Tenth Yearbook of the National Council of Teachers of Mathematics).* New York: Columbia University, Teachers College, Bureau of Publications, pp. 1–31.

Brownell, W. A. (1987). AT Classic: Meaning and Skill—Maintaining the Balance. *Arithmetic Teacher,* 34(8), 18–25. (Original work published 1956).

Devlin, K. (2000). Finding Your Inner Mathematician. *The Chronicle of Higher Education,* 46, B5.

Henry, V. & Brown, R. (2008). First-Grade Basic Facts: An Investigation into Teaching and Learning of an Accelerated, High-Demand Memorization Standards. *Journal for Research in Mathematics Education,* 399(2), 153–183.

Isaacs, A. C. & Carroll, W. M. (1999). Strategies for Basic-Facts Instruction. *Teaching Children Mathematics,* 5(9), 508–515.

Janvier, C. (1987). *Problems of Representation in the Teaching and Learning of Mathematic.* NJ: Lawrence Erlbaum Associates.

Kilpatrick, J., Swafford, J. & Findell, B. (2001). *Adding It Up: Helping Children Learn Mathematics.* Washington, DC: National Academy Press.

Lesh, R., Post, T., & Behr, M. (1987). Representations and Translations among Representations in Mathematics Learning and Problem Solving. In C. Janvier, (Ed.), *Problems of Representations in the Teaching and Learning of Mathematics*. Hillsdale, NJ: Lawrence Erlbaum, pp. 33–40.

Logan, G. D. (1991). Automaticity and Memory. In W. E. Hockley & S. Lewandowsky (Eds.), *Relating Theory and Data: Essays on Human Memory in Honor of Bennet B*. Hillsdale, NJ: Lawrence Erlbaum Associates.

Maccini, P. & Gagnon, J. C. (2000). Best Practices for Teaching Mathematics to Secondary Students with Special Needs. *Focus on Exceptional Children*, 32, 1–21.

National Council of Teachers of Mathematics. (2000). *Principles and Standards for School Mathematics*. Reston, VA: National Council of Teachers of Mathematics.

National Governors Association for Best Practices and the Council of Chief State School Officers. (2010). *Common Core State Standards for Mathematics*. Retrieved on June 15, 2018 from http://www.corestandards.org/Math/

Newton, R. (2016). Math Running Records. Routledge: NY

Pape, S. & Tchoshanov, M. (2001). The Role of Representations(s) in Developing Mathematical Understanding. *Theory into Practice*, 40(2), 118–127.

Sherin, B. & Fuson, K. (2005). Multiplication Strategies and the Appropriation of Computational Resources. *Journal for Research in Mathematics Education*, 336(4), 347–395.

Van de Walle, John A. (2001). *Elementary and Middle School Mathematics: Teaching Developmentally* (4th ed.). New York: Addison Wesley Longman, Inc.

Van de Walle, John A. (2004). *Elementary and Middle School Mathematics* (5th ed.). New York: Addison Wesley Longman, Inc.

Van de Walle, John A. (2007). *Elementary and Middle School Mathematics: Teaching Developmentally*. Boston: Pearson, Allyn and Bacon.

Vygotsky, L. S. (1978). *Mind in Society: The Development of Higher Psychological Processes*. Cambridge, MA: Harvard University Press.

8

Word Problem Workstations

Problem solving is way more than merely getting an answer!

Problem Solving Throughout Math Workshop

Problem solving should take place throughout Math workshop (see Figure 8.1). There should be a problem-solving routine every day where students work on a problem as a whole class to talk about big ideas, do think alouds around strategies and models and discuss various solutions. It doesn't have to be a different problem every day; it should be a focus on problem solving and working through the practice of problem solving—reading the problem, making sure that everyone understands the problems, making a plan, solving one way and checking another and then double-double checking (the model, the equation and the answer) to see if everything addresses the problem. In small groups, teachers work with groups on developing a deeper understanding of problem types and solutions. In the workstations, students work on the problem types that they are ready for. As Buchanan and Helman, note, "Individual work settings ensure that all students process lessons at their own rate of learning" (2000).

Figure 8.1 Word Problems

Big Ideas	Enduring Understandings
There are 15 single step and five two-step problems. Most state standards require that kindergarteners know two to four types, that first graders know the rest. By second grade all the types for all the categories and the two-step problems should be mastered.	Word problems are about different types of situations. There are four basic types of situations: add to, take from, part-part whole and compare. By second grade they should start working on the five types of two-step word problems.
Essential Questions How do we solve word problems? What are different strategies that we could use? What are different models that we could use?	Know/Do Students should be able to solve various types of problems using a variety of models. They should be able to talk about what type of problem they are solving and name their strategies. Students should be able to write a symbol for the missing number in the problem.

Some Word Problems Are Easy and Others Aren't!

Word problems have a hierarchy. The idea that we should teach them according to this hierarchy from easy to more challenging has been around in the research for a long time.

(Carpenter et al., 1999)

However, in our everyday practice, it seems to get lost. We end up teaching our students all the levels just jumbled together, more often than not, never checking if they have mastered the easier levels before we go on to the more difficult ones.

Research notes that "Teaching the progression of problem types is essential, and when problems are taught from easier to more difficult using explicit instruction with multiple representations, students attain higher achievement levels" (Pfannenstiel, Bryant, Bryant and Porterfield, 2015).

The types of word problems and the grade level at which they are introduced is in every state's core standards. But, just because it is there, doesn't mean we use it to build strong foundations for problem solving. To compound this kind of present-day, randomly chaotic approach to teaching word problems, in K and first grade it becomes even trickier because many of the students are just learning to read. So, there has to be easily accessible problems for the students. This can be done with word problems that are read to the students and word problems that have visual clues. The word problem workstations should be clearly scaffolded from easy to more difficult around what the students have to know by the end of their grade (see Figures 8.2 and 8.3).

Figure 8.2 Grade Level Responsibilities

K Problems	First Grade Problems	Second Grade Problems
2 to 4 types of problems	11 to 15 types of problems	All 15 problems and five two-step stories

Figure 8.3 Types of Problems

The Leveled Workstations are based on the problem types that students have to know (Carpenter et al., 1999).

Join/Separate	Result Unknown	Change Unknown	Start Unknown
Join	Marta had five marbles. She got two more. How many does she have now? $5 + 2 = ?$	Marta had five marbles. She got some more. Now she has seven. How many did she get? $5 + ? = 7$ $7 - 5 = ?$	Marta had some marbles. She got two more. Now she has five. How many did she have in the beginning? $? + 2 = 5$ $5 - 2 = ?$
Separate	Joe had ten marbles. He gave two to his brother. How many does he have left? $10 - 2 = ?$	Joe had ten marbles. He gave some to his friends. Now he has five left. How many did he give away? $10 - ? = 5$ $5 + ? = 10$	Joe had some marbles. He gave three away. Now he has seven. How many did he have in the beginning? $? - 3 = 7$ or $3 + 7 = 10$
Part-Part Whole	**Whole Unknown**	**Both Addends Unknown**	**Part Unknown**
Part-Part Whole	Jamal had three big marbles and four small marbles. How many did he have altogether? $3 + 4 = 7$	Jamal had seven marbles. Some were big and some were small. How many of each could he have? $7 + 0; 6 + 1; 5 + 2;$ $4 + 3; 3 + 4; 2 + 5; 1 + 6;$ $0 + 7$	Jamal had seven marbles. Three were big. The rest were small. How many were small? $7 - 3 = ?$ $3 + \_\_ = 7$
Compare	**Difference** **Easy Version**	**Bigger Part Unknown** **Easy Version**	**Smaller Part Unknown** **Easy Version**
Compare	Grace had seven rings. Lucy had four. How many more marbles did Grace have than Lucy? $7 - 4 = ?$ $4 + \_\_\_ = 7$	Lucy had four rings. Grace had three more than she did. How many did Grace have? $4 + 3 = ?$	Grace had seven rings. Lucy had three less than she did. How many did Lucy have? $7 - 3 = ?$
	Difference **Harder Version**	**Bigger Part Unknown** **Harder Version**	**Smaller Part Unknown** **Harder Version**
Compare	Grace had seven rings. Lucy had four. How many fewer marbles did Lucy have than Grace ? $7 - 4 = ?$	Lucy had four rings. She had three less than Grace. How many did Grace have? $? - 3 = 4$ or $4 + 3 = ?$	Grace had seven rings. She had three more than Lucy. How many did Lucy have? $7 - 3 = ?$

K Leveled Workstations

- **Level 1: Add to Result Unknown**

  Marta had five marbles. She got five more. How many does she have altogether?

- **Level 2: Take From Result Unknown**

  Luke had seven marbles. He gave away five. How many does he have left?

- **Level 3: Part-Part Whole Whole Unknown**

  Mary had three pink rings and two yellow rings. How many rings did she have altogether?

- **Level 4: Part-Part Whole Both Addends Unknown**

  Jojo had five marbles. Some were yellow and some were green. How many of each did he have?

Inside the Workstations

There should be bags, boxes or word problem booklets with these types of problems. Students should have to work through about ten of these problems at the concrete, pictorial and abstract level. Students should provide evidence of their work. There could be templates, story mats, retelling mats etc.

TEMPLATES

Students work through a workbook on the problem types where they have to use various templates (see Figures 8.4 and 8.5).

Figure 8.4 Word Problems with Pictures

Figure 8.5 Word Problems with Rekenreks

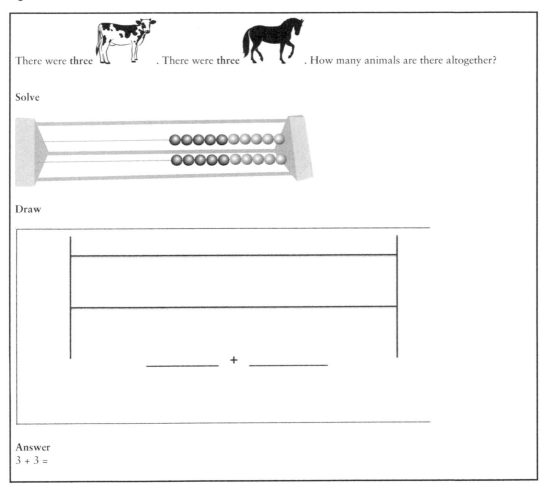

There were **three** 🐄 . There were **three** 🐎 . How many animals are there altogether?

Solve

Draw

_____ + _____

Answer
3 + 3 =

STORY PROBLEM MATS

Story Problem Mats are great because they have pictures. Students can use the pictures to describe and solve the story (see Figure 8.6).

Figure 8.6 Word Problem Mats

RETELLING MATS

Students work with puppets and mats to retell familiar stories and make up new ones using the same context. Students can use storytelling sticks and bags and necklaces as well. They can also pull an expression or equation and act it out (see Figures 8.7 and 8.8).

Figure 8.7 Word Problem Mat with Puppets

Figure 8.8 Expressions To Use for Word Problem Mats

5 – 1	4 – 2	3 – 3	4 – 3	1 – 1

First Grade Leveled Workstations (first use the kindergarten ones for review and make sure students who haven't mastered those levels continue to practice the levels that they don't know).

- **Level 5: Add to Change Unknown**

  Sue had five marbles. She got some more. Now she has seven marbles. How many did she get?

- **Level 6: Take From Change Unknown**

  Mike had ten Marbles. He gave some away. Now he has seven left. How many did he give away?

- **Level 7: Part-Part Part Unknown**

  Jamal had 12 marbles. Five were blue. The rest were green. How many were green?

- **Level 8: Compare Difference Unknown (More)**

  Mario had five marbles. Joe had three. How many more did Mario have?

- **Level 9: Compare Difference Unknown (Less)**

  Lucy had 20 marbles. Mary had 18. How many fewer marbles did Mary have than Lucy.

- **Level 10: Compare Bigger Part Unknown**

  Jessica had seven marbles. Marta had three more than she did. How many did Marta have?

- **Level 11: Compare Smaller Part Unknown**

  Manda had 12 marbles. Terri had two fewer marbles than Manda. How many marbles did Terri have?

Inside the Workstations

There should be bags, boxes or word problem booklets with these types of problems. Students should have to work through about ten of each of these problems at the concrete, pictorial and abstract level. Students should have evidence of their work. Students should have the opportunity to practice with counters, bears, cubes, rekenreks, ten frames, drawings and using templates.

TEMPLATES

Students work through a workbook on the problem types where they have to use various templates (see Figure 8.9).

Figure 8.9 Word Problem Templates

Joe had seven marbles. Mike had five. How many more did Joe have than Mike? Write an equation with a symbol for the unknown part. _____ ☐ _____ = _____ Solve on the double ten frame. Answer: _____	Marta had ten marbles. She gave away seven. How many does she have left? Write an equation with a symbol for the unknown part. _____ ☐ _____ = _____ Draw a picture: Answer: _____

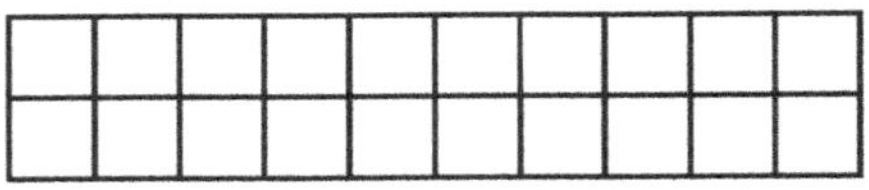

The bakery had 20 cupcakes. They sold 14. How many do they have left?

Write an equation with a symbol for the unknown part.

_____ ☐ _____ = _____

Use the number line to model your thinking.

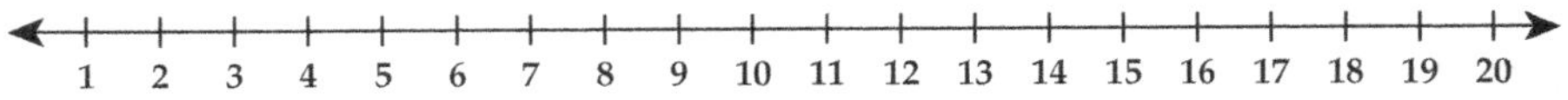

1 2 3 4 5 6 7 8 9 10 11 12 13 14 15 16 17 18 19 20

Answer: _____

STORY PROBLEM MATS

Word Problem Mats excite and motivate students to tell and solve stories. (see Figures 8.10 and 8.11).

Figure 8.10 Word Problem Mats

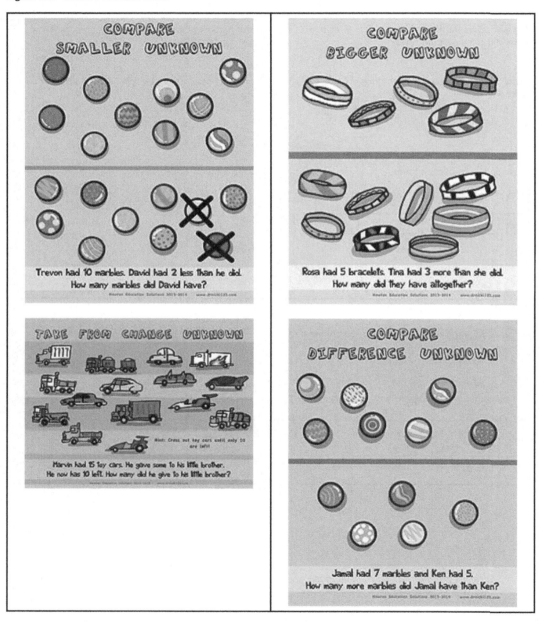

Template Booklets (see my Problem Solving with Math Models Books)

Figure 8.11 Template Examples

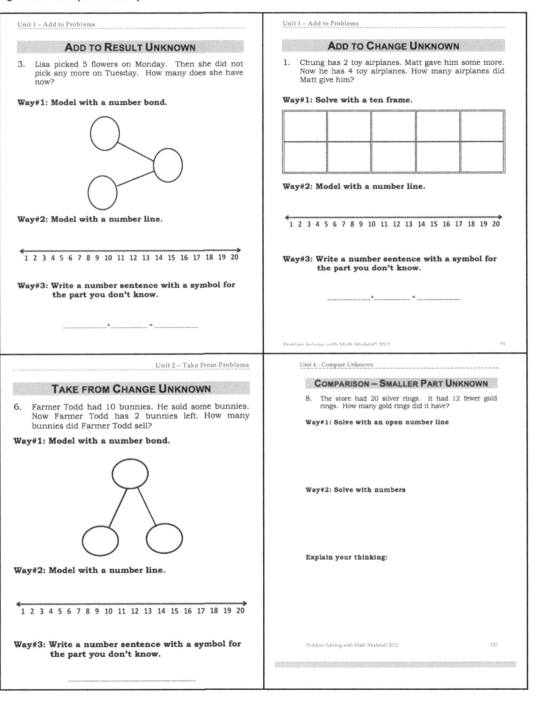

Unit 1 – Add to Problems

ADD TO RESULT UNKNOWN

3. Lisa picked 5 flowers on Monday. Then she did not pick any more on Tuesday. How many does she have now?

Way#1: Model with a number bond.

Way#2: Model with a number line.

1 2 3 4 5 6 7 8 9 10 11 12 13 14 15 16 17 18 19 20

Way#3: Write a number sentence with a symbol for the part you don't know.

_____+_____ = _____

Unit 1 – Add to Problems

ADD TO CHANGE UNKNOWN

1. Chung has 2 toy airplanes. Matt gave him some more. Now he has 4 toy airplanes. How many airplanes did Matt give him?

Way#1: Solve with a ten frame.

Way#2: Model with a number line.

1 2 3 4 5 6 7 8 9 10 11 12 13 14 15 16 17 18 19 20

Way#3: Write a number sentence with a symbol for the part you don't know.

_____+_____ = _____

Problem Solving with Math Models© 2012   23

Unit 2 – Take From Problems

TAKE FROM CHANGE UNKNOWN

6. Farmer Todd had 10 bunnies. He sold some bunnies. Now Farmer Todd has 2 bunnies left. How many bunnies did Farmer Todd sell?

Way#1: Model with a number bond.

Way#2: Model with a number line.

1 2 3 4 5 6 7 8 9 10 11 12 13 14 15 16 17 18 19 20

Way#3: Write a number sentence with a symbol for the part you don't know.

_____

Unit 4 – Compare Unknown

COMPARISON – SMALLER PART UNKNOWN

8. The store had 20 silver rings. It had 12 fewer gold rings. How many gold rings did it have?

Way#1: Solve with an open number line

Way#2: Solve with numbers

Explain your thinking:

Problem Solving with Math Models© 2012   125

SECOND GRADE LEVELED WORKSTATIONS

First use the first grade ones for review and make sure students who haven't mastered those levels continue to practice the levels that they don't know. Also, in some states the students have to learn all the problem types in first grade.

- **Level 12: Compare Bigger Part Unknown (Harder Version: you say fewer but you are looking for the larger)**

  Joe had 12 marbles. He had two fewer than Luis. How many did Luis have?

- **Level 13: Compare Smaller Part Unknown (Harder Version: you say more but you are looking for the smaller part)**

  Sue had five marbles. She had two more than Lana. How many did Lana have?

- **Level 14: Add to Start Unknown**

  Tom had some marbles. He got five more. Now he has ten. How many did he have in the beginning?

- **Level 15: Take From Start Unknown**

  Maria had some marbles. She gave four away. Now she has six. How many did she have in the beginning?

Five Multistep Problems

- **Level 1: Multiple Steps but One Operation**

  Sue had five marbles. She got seven more. Then, she got two more. How many did she get altogether?

- **Level 2: Two Steps but Two Operations**

  Marco had five marbles. He gave two to his brother. His mother gave him three more. How many does he have now?

- **Level 3: Two Steps but Easy Mixed Levels**

  Larry had five marbles. Jamal had two more than he did. How many did they have altogether?

- **Level 4: Two Steps Medium Version of Mixed Levels**

  There were three chickens and some ducks. There were six animals altogether. Then, two more ducks came. How many ducks were there altogether?

- **Level 5: Two Steps Hard Version of Mixed Levels**

  There were three chickens and some ducks. There were six animals altogether. Then some more ducks came. Now there are ten ducks. How many more ducks came?

Inside the Workstations

There should be bags, boxes or word problem booklets with these types of problems. Students should have to work through about ten of these problems at the concrete, pictorial and abstract level. Students should have evidence of their work.

In the first part of the second grade use word problem bags when reviewing the first grade types of problems, the progression should be from easy numbers within 10 to numbers within 20 and then 100. In the second part of the word problem bags are the harder versions, depending on your state. The third part of the word problem bags is the two-step problems.

*Second grade focuses on mastering all the 15 single-step problems with numbers up to 100. Then, they work on two-step problems.

TEMPLATES

Students work through a workbook on the problem types where they have to use various templates (see Figures 8.12 and 8.13).

Figure 8.12 Second Grade Template Examples

Joe had 52 marbles. Mike had 33. How many more did Joe have than Mike? Write an equation with a symbol for the unknown part. _____ + _____ = _____ Model your thinking with the base ten blocks: hundred Answer: _	The bakery had 40 blueberry cupcakes. They had 15 fewer cherry cupcakes. How many cherry cupcakes did they have? Write an equation with a symbol for the unknown part. _____ + _____ = _____ Model your thinking with the number line:

1	2	3	4	5	6	7	8	9	10
11	12	13	14	15	16	17	18	19	20
21	22	23	24	25	26	27	28	29	30
31	32	33	34	35	36	37	38	39	40
41	42	43	44	45	46	47	48	49	50
51	52	53	54	55	56	57	58	59	60
61	62	63	64	65	66	67	68	69	70
71	72	73	74	75	76	77	78	79	80
81	82	83	84	85	86	87	88	89	90
91	92	93	94	95	96	97	98	99	100

_____

We could count back 15.

Answer: _____

*Math Learning Center Virtual Manipulatives

The bakery had 53 cupcakes. They sold 39. How many do they have left?

Write an equation with a symbol for the unknown part.

_____ + _____ = _____

Use the open number line to model your thinking.

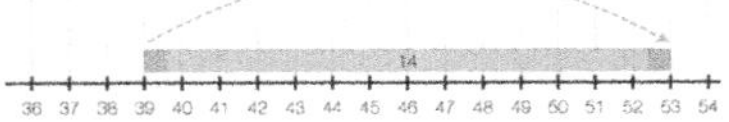

You could count up from 30 to 53. The difference is 14.

Answer: _____

STORY PROBLEM MATS

Word Problem Mats are great because they have pictures. Students can use the pictures to describe and solve the story (see Figure 8.13).

Figure 8.13 More Story Problem Mats

Template Booklets (see my Problem Solving with Math Models (Newton, 2018) examples Figure 8.14)

Figure 8.14 Template Examples

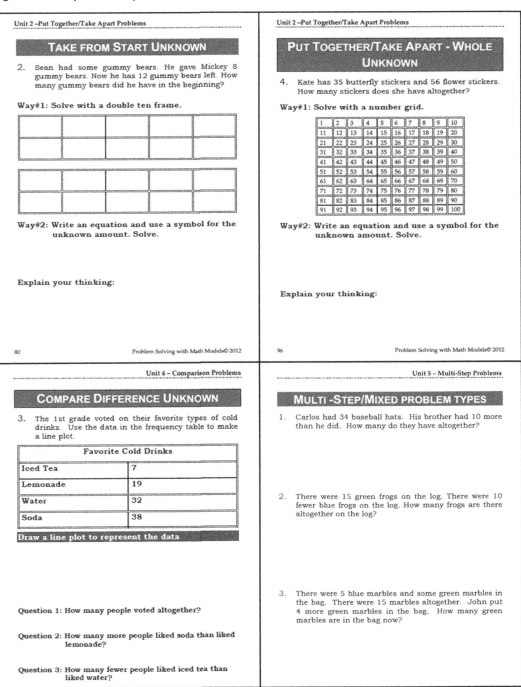

Unit 2 –Put Together/Take Apart Problems

TAKE FROM START UNKNOWN

2. Sean had some gummy bears. He gave Mickey 8 gummy bears. Now he has 12 gummy bears left. How many gummy bears did he have in the beginning?

Way#1: Solve with a double ten frame.

Way#2: Write an equation and use a symbol for the unknown amount. Solve.

Explain your thinking:

80   Problem Solving with Math Models© 2012

Unit 2 –Put Together/Take Apart Problems

PUT TOGETHER/TAKE APART - WHOLE UNKNOWN

4. Kate has 35 butterfly stickers and 56 flower stickers. How many stickers does she have altogether?

Way#1: Solve with a number grid.

1	2	3	4	5	6	7	8	9	10
11	12	13	14	15	16	17	18	19	20
21	22	23	24	25	26	27	28	29	30
31	32	33	34	35	36	37	38	39	40
41	42	43	44	45	46	47	48	49	50
51	52	53	54	55	56	57	58	59	60
61	62	63	64	65	66	67	68	69	70
71	72	73	74	75	76	77	78	79	80
81	82	83	84	85	86	87	88	89	90
91	92	93	94	95	96	97	98	99	100

Way#2: Write an equation and use a symbol for the unknown amount. Solve.

Explain your thinking:

96   Problem Solving with Math Models© 2012

Unit 4 – Comparison Problems

COMPARE DIFFERENCE UNKNOWN

3. The 1st grade voted on their favorite types of cold drinks. Use the data in the frequency table to make a line plot.

Favorite Cold Drinks	
Iced Tea	7
Lemonade	19
Water	32
Soda	38

Draw a line plot to represent the data

Question 1: How many people voted altogether?

Question 2: How many more people liked soda than liked lemonade?

Question 3: How many fewer people liked iced tea than liked water?

Unit 5 – Multi-Step Problems

MULTI -STEP/MIXED PROBLEM TYPES

1. Carlos had 34 baseball hats. His brother had 10 more than he did. How many do they have altogether?

2. There were 15 green frogs on the log. There were 10 fewer blue frogs on the log. How many frogs are there altogether on the log?

3. There were 5 blue marbles and some green marbles in the bag. There were 15 marbles altogether. John put 4 more green marbles in the bag. How many green marbles are in the bag now?

Keeping Students Accountable

Students should record their thinking on the different recording sheets shown throughout the chapter. Students should have their own word problem folder where they can keep their ongoing work. It is important to have templates in the beginning to scaffold and record student thinking. These templates should have spaces for students to visualize, summarize, make a plan, solve one way and check another and double-double check their work. Eventually, we want students to be able to solve problems without the template, so it should be faded out as the year progresses.

NCTM (2000) process standards state that students should:

- Create and use representations to organize, record and communicate mathematical ideas
- Select, apply and translate among mathematical representations to solve problems
- Use representations to model and interpret physical, social and mathematical phenomena

Keeping Track of It All

It is essential that at the beginning of the year we give students a word problem test so that we know their entry level of understanding. They should take the assessment from the grade before to make sure that they have mastered all of the types from the grade level before because word problems are a hierarchy and you shouldn't be working on a level 8 if you can't solve a level 1.

As the grades go higher, students are working with larger number ranges for each problem type. So, although you give the first grade test, you still work with those problem types but now with higher numbers. If students are having trouble with the problem type with lower numbers then you won't do it with higher numbers. Teachers should be collecting individual student data and then class data. The data should be reviewed across the grade band as well.

Helping Parents/Guardians Help Their Children

First Grade Example (see Figure 8.15)

Figure 8.15 Parent/Guardian Letter

Dear Parents/Guardians!

We are working on word problems. We are sending home a word problem mat. There are different types of word problems. Altogether there are 11 different types of word problems in first grade. Your child is working on level 5. In this level we are working on Add to Change Unknown problems. In this type of problem we are looking at a situation where the change (the middle part of the story) is unknown. That means there was something and then something happened and we don't know what but there was a change. For example: There were four dogs in the park. Some more came. Now there are ten dogs in the park. How many dogs came?

There are several ways to solve this problem. We are sending home three different ways to model the problem. Please use the paper mosaics to act out the problem. Also practice this problem using drawings and number lines.

Way 1: Ten frame

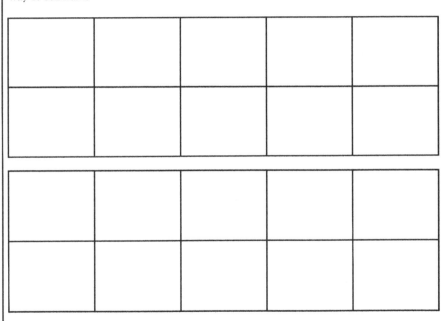

Way 2: Drawing (have the student do a quick draw—circles etc.)

Way 3: Number Line

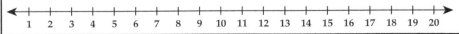

Assessment

Check drnickinewton.com under the K–2 problem-solving book for other sample tests (see Figures 8.16 and 8.17).

Here is an example of a final kindergarten word problem test.

Figure 8.16 Word Problem Assessment

1. There were four dogs and four cats. How many animals were there altogether?

   A. Model in the ten frame:

   B. Answer _____

2. There were five horses in the field and three left. How many horses are there now in the field?

   A. Model with a drawing:

   B. Answer: _____

3. Jamal had three blue marbles and three orange marbles. How many marbles did he have altogether?

   A. Model your thinking.

   B. Answer: _____

4. There are four marbles in a box. Some are orange and some are yellow. Draw how many different ways the marbles could be in the box.

a.	b.	c.	d.	e.

Figure 8.17 More Examples of Word Problem Assessments

1st Grade End of the Year Benchmark Word Problems

Name: _____   Date: _____

1.) Luke had 5 marbles. His dad gave him some more. Now he has 7. How many did his dad give him?
   a. Model your thinking.

   b. Write a number sentence for the problem that shows where the missing number is.

   _____ • _____ = _____

   c. Answer: _____ marbles

2.) Maria had 10 rings. She gave her sister some. Now she only has 5 left. How many did she give to her sister?
   a.) Use the drawing below to model your thinking.

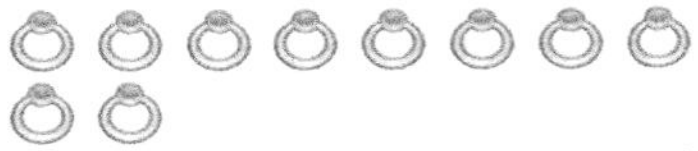

   ⊚ ⊚ ⊚ ⊚ ⊚ ⊚ ⊚ ⊚
   ⊚ ⊚

   b.) Write a number sentence for the problem that shows where the missing number is.

   _____ • _____ = _____

   c.) Answer: _____ rings

3.) In the house there were 12 children. Six children were upstairs. How many children were down stairs?
   a.) Model your thinking.

   b.) Write a number sentence for the problem that shows where the missing number is.

   _____ • _____ = _____

   c.) Answer: _____ children

4.) Marvin has 9 toy cars. Leo has 3. How many **fewer** toy cars does Leo have than Marvin?
   a.) Model your thinking.

   b.) Answer: _____ fewer toy cars

5.) Sharon has 5 cookies. Mary has 1 more than she does. How many cookies does Mary have?
   a.) Model your thinking.

6.) Jason has 4 lollipops. Greg has 1 fewer lollipops than Jason. How many lollipops does Greg have?
   a.) Model your thinking.

   b.) Answer: _____ cookies

7.) Kelly has 7 necklaces and Jane has 5 necklaces. How many **more** necklaces does Kelly have than Jane?
   a.) Model your thinking.

   b.) Answer: _____more necklaces

8.) Mike had 9 red marbles, 2 blue marbles and 1 green one. How many marbles did he have altogether?
   a.) Model your thinking.

   b.) Answer: _____ marbles altogether

Goal Setting

Figure 8.18 Goal Setting

I Can Solve Different Types of Word Problems.			
Add to	Take From	Part-Part Whole	Compare
 ⭐ ⭐	 ⭐ ⭐	 ⭐ ⭐ ⭐	 ⭐ ⭐ ⭐

Figure 8.19 Class Snapshot

1	2	3
Today I didn't work very hard. I did not do what I was supposed to do. Tomorrow I will do better! 	Today I did some of my work. I was off task some of the time. 	I worked really well today. I did all my work. 

Figure 8.20 Tracking Class Data

	L1	L2	L3	L4	L5	L6	L7	L8	L9	L10	L11
Luke	x										
Tom	x										
Maritza	x										
Kelly		x									
Susie		x									
Joe			x								
Mary			x								
Kiyana			x								
Shakhira				x							
Marcus				x							
Greg					x						
Zeke					x						

Figure 8.21 Getting Started

Getting Started!

There are some great resources for teachers to use to get started. Here are three:

1. Greg Tang Word Problem Generator: He has organized all the word problem types by category. You can work with the website either as a whole class or in workstations. Teachers can also make a list of the problem types and put them in the workstation. If done on the website, models are given. http://gregtangmath.com/wordproblems
2. South Dakota CGI: They have all the word problems by type in a document on their website. Organized but no models are given.

Google: [PDF]CGI Problems—South Dakota ESA

3. I am in the middle of a project to make PowerPoint slides for all the word problem types and organize them by level. There are four problems for each level. Students would use a workmat to solve the problems. I also have word problem books that can be used. The PowerPoint slides are made from these books. The books have 8 to 12 problems per type.

Word Problem Mats: *https://gigglenookmathstore.com/pages/word-problem-story-mats*
Word Problem Books:

Word Problem PowerPoints: See www.drnickinewton.com/

Researcher	Research	Big Ideas	How Does This Research Inform Our Practice?
Jitendra, A. K., Griffin, C. C., Haria, P., Leh, J., Adams, A., & Kaduvettoor, A. (2007). A Comparison of Single and Multiple Strategy Instruction on Third-Grade Students' Mathematical Problem Solving. *Journal of Educational Psychology*, 99, 115–127. Jitendra, A. K., Griffin, C. C., McGoey, K., Gardill, M. C., Bhat, P., & Riley, T. (1998). Effects of Mathematical Word Problem Solving By Students at Risk or With Mild Disabilities. *The Journal of Educational Research*, 91, 345–355. Leh, J. M., & Jitendra, A. K. (2013). Effects of Computer-Mediated Versus Teacher-Mediated Instruction On the Mathematical Word Problem-Solving Performance of Third-Grade Students With Mathematical Difficulties. *Learning Disability Quarterly*, 36, 68–79. Gersten, R., Beckmann, S., Clarke, B., Foegen, A., Marsha, L., Star, J. R., & Witzel, B. (2009). Assisting Students Struggling With Mathematics: Response to Intervention (RtI) for Elementary and Middle School (NCEE 2009–4060). Washington, DC: National Center for Educational Evaluation and Regional Assistance, Institute of Education Sciences, U.S. Department of Education.	Explicit instruction on word problems improves students' achievement.	Researchers found that a step-by-step, teacher modeling and then students modeling, immediate feedback cycle for teaching word problems improves students' understanding of word problems. Explicit instruction in recognizing the types of word problems, representing them, and finding and using a solution strategy improves student achievement.	It is really important to make sure that students have had the explicit instruction around word problems before they go to independent practice. How do you plan for this?
Fuchs, L. S., Seethaler, P. M., Powell, S. R., Fuchs, D., & Hamlett, C. L. (2008). Effects of Preventative Tutoring On the Mathematical Problem Solving of Third-Grade Students With Math and Reading Difficulties. *Exceptional Children*, 74, 155–173. Fuchs, L. S., Fuchs, D., Craddock, C., Hollenbeck, K. N., Hamlett, C. L., & Schatschneider, C. (2008). Effects of Small-Group Tutoring With and Without Validated Classroom Instruction On At-Risk Students' Math Problem Solving: Are Two Tiers of Prevention Better Than One? *Journal of Educational Psychology*, 100. Gersten, R., Beckmann, S., Clarke, B., Foegen, A., Marsha, L., Star, J. R., & Witzel, B. (2009). Assisting Students Struggling With Mathematics: Response to Intervention (RtI) for Elementary and Middle School (NCEE 2009–4060). Washington, DC: National Center for Educational Evaluation and Regional Assistance, Institute of Education Sciences, U.S. Department of Education.	Knowing the problem type is very important.	Researchers taught students how to identify and name the different problem types. They practiced solving the problems with "concrete examples and role playing through explicit instruction." The researchers also used posters about each problem type that had "specific steps" for solving that problem type (Fuchs, Seethaler, Powerll, Fuchs, & Hamlett 2008).	Are your workstations set up by problem type, organized from easiest to most difficult?

Researcher	Research	Big Ideas	How Does This Research Inform Our Practice?
Fuchs, L. S., Fuchs, D., Craddock, C., Hollenbeck, K. N., Hamlett, C. L., & Schatschneider, C. (2008). Effects of Small-Group Tutoring With and Without Validated Classroom Instruction On At-Risk Students' Math Problem Solving: Are Two Tiers of Prevention Better Than One? *Journal of Educational Psychology*, 100, 491–509. Cassel, J., & Reid, R. (1996). Use of a Self-Regulated Strategy Intervention to Improve Word Problem-Solving Skills of Students With Mild Disabilities. *Journal of Behavioral Education*, 6, 153–172.	Self-monitoring strategies can be very effective.	Researchers have found that a variety of self-learning strategies such as learning contracts, self-monitoring strategy checklists, student-monitored graphs, setting personal goals and students checking their answer with an answer key positively impact student learning.	In what ways do your students use self-monitoring strategies around the work they do in math workstations?
Kingsdorf, S., Krawec, J., & Gritter, K. (2016). A Broad Look at the Literature on Math Word Problem-solving Interventions for Third Graders, 3(1). Retrieved on September 19, 2018 from www.tandfonline.com/doi/full/10.1080/2331186X.2015.1135770	Visual representations are important.	Researchers found that visual representations are an important part of solving word problems. However it is recommended that this is coupled with self-monitoring strategies so that students can reflect on how the model is helping them solve the problem and if it makes sense.	What is the role of visual representations in your word problem workstation? Are students expected to model their thinking in more than one way?

Key Points

- Schema-Based Problems
- CGI
- Kindergarten Does Four Problems
- First Grade Does 11 to 15 Problems
- Second Grade Does Four Harder Version Problems and Five Two-Step Problems
- Parent Packet

Summary

Leveled word problem workstations help to scaffold student access to word problems. There is a hierarchy of word problem types. Students should go step by step and master the levels in order when they are practicing. In the general class discussions students will work with all types of problems, but when they are practicing in their zone of proximal development they should work where they are and progress as they do. It's pretty straightforward in terms of leveling the stations. There should be a bag for each level with about 8 to 10 opportunities for students to work with the problems in concrete, pictorial and abstract ways. There are so many resources available to start the work and I encourage teachers to use them (see Figures 8.20 and 8.21).

Reflection Questions

1. What is one thing that stands out for you in this chapter?
2. Are you currently framing your word problem work for the entire year around the word problem levels?
3. How are you scaffolding parent involvement so that it is meaningful?

References

Buchanan, K. & Helman, M. (2000). *Reforming Mathematics Instruction for ESL Literacy Students*. http://files.eric.ed.gov/fulltext/ED414769.pdf. September 20, 2018.

Carpenter, T. P., Fennema, E., Franke, M. L., Levi, L. & Empson, S. B. (1999). *Children's Mathematics: Cognitively Guided Instruction*. Portsmouth, NH: Heinemann.

National Council of Teachers of Mathematics. (2000). *Principles and Standards for School Mathematics*. Reston, VA: National Council of Teachers of Mathematics.

Newton, R. (2018). *Problem Solving with Math Models*. Connecticut: Gigglenook.

Pfannenstiel, K. H., Bryant, D., Bryant, B. & Porterfield, J. (2015). Cognitive Strategy Instruction for Teaching Word Problems to Primary-Level Struggling Students. *Intervention in School and Clinic*, 50(5), 291–296. Hammill Institute on Disabilities.

9

Action Planning

It doesn't get done unless you start doing it.

There is a good deal of evidence that learning is enhanced when teachers pay attention to the knowledge and beliefs that learners bring to a learning task, use this knowledge as a starting point for new instruction, and monitor students' changing conceptions as instruction proceeds.

—(Bransford et al., 1999, p. 11)

Start

You just have to start. You have to have a plan (see Figures 9.1–9.4). You have to have some dates. You have to follow your plan, reflect on the plan and revise the plan. In order to get started you want to think about and focus on the grade level fluency. Start by creating workstations that address the specified grade level fluency and make sure there is at least one game at the concrete, pictorial and abstract level for each type of fact. After that is done well, then add games for the range of facts that students work with in that grade level. For example, in kindergarten the fluency is within 5 but the fact range is within 10 so first get the workstations up for the fluency and then later focus on adding games within the fact range.

Figure 9.1 Planning Questions A

Goals: Where do you want to start?	Tasks: What do you need to do to make that happen? What is step 1? What is step 2? What is step 3?	Success Criteria: What does success look like? When you succeed, how will you know?	Time Frame: What is your time frame? When will you get started? When do you want to have achieved your goal?	Resources: What do you need to make this happen? What do people need to do? What physical resources do you need?

Figure 9.2 Planning Questions B

Cross Grade View	Focus Area	Goals: What Specifically Do We Want to Do?	Timeline: When?	Actions: What Will It Take to Get It Done?	Review: How Are We Doing?	Revise: What Is Next?
	Fluency	Leveled workstations within the grade level fluency range	First Year	Find/Make Stations for Each Level	What is working? What do we need to improve?	Revise Current Stations and then think about adding at least one more game at the concrete, pictorial and abstract level.
K		Leveled workstations within 5: At least one concrete, one pictorial and one abstract game				
First		Workstations within 10: At least one concrete, one pictorial and one abstract game				
Second		Workstations within 20: At least one concrete, one pictorial and one abstract game				

Figure 9.3 Planning Questions C

Cross Grade View	Focus Area	Goals: What Specifically Do We Want to Do?	Timeline: When?	Actions: What Will It Take to Get It Done?	Review: How Are We Doing?	Revise: What Is Next?
	Word Problems	Leveled workstations within the word problem range	First Year	Find/Make Stations for Each Level	What is working? What do we need to improve?	Revise Current Stations and then think about adding at least one more game at the concrete, pictorial and abstract level.
K		Four types of K word problems				
First		K + additional seven types of first grade problems				
Second		K, first and then the four other single-step second grade problems and the five levels of second grade multi-step word problems				

Figure 9.4 Planning Questions D

Cross Grade View	Focus Area	Goals: What Specifically Do We Want to Do?	Timeline: When?	Actions: What Will It Take to Get It Done?	Review: How Are We Doing?	Revise: What Is Next?
	Place Value	At least one concrete, one pictorial and one abstract game	First Year	Find/Make Stations for Each Level	What is working? What do we need to improve?	Revise Current Stations and then think about adding at least one more game at the concrete, pictorial and abstract level.
K		K activities				
First		K games + add first grade games.				
Second		Put in first grade games and then slowly add second grade games as concepts are introduced.				

Reference

Bransford, J., Brown, A. L., Cocking, R. R., & National Research Council (U.S.). (1999). *How People Learn: Brain, Mind, Experience, and School*. Washington, DC: National Research Council.

Frequently Asked Questions

1. **When do I start workstations?** You should start introducing them during the first 20 days. Start slow. You may only start with one or two for a few weeks or months. Do one well and then introduce another. In kindergarten, start with geometry, counting and numbers. Not all at once; one at a time. Introduce each station to the whole class at the easiest level. In this way, everyone learns the basics. Play together and practice a great deal. Then, when you want to introduce a differentiation aspect, pull a small group and do that.

2. **How many times a week should students go to workstations?** This really depends on your schedule. Some people go every day while others only do it once a week. I think ideally you do workstations at least three or four times a week, the same time that you are doing guided math groups.

3. **How do I know who goes where?** This is the key to doing workstations well. You have to have some good, actionable data so you know where to place the students. It is important to test students in the priority areas at the beginning of the year from the past year because what they left the prior grade knowing doesn't necessarily mean they come into the current grade knowing those same things.

4. **How do I know if they are really doing the work?** It is important to have students record their work. This can be done on recording sheets or students can just write down what they are doing in their journals. They can also use different apps to record their work and discuss it (such as Seesaw etc.).

5. **How many workstations should I have?** Personal sanity is at a premium at all times. That being said, four or five at the most. You should have a fluency, word problem and place value workstation from the very beginning in first and second grade and by the end of the year in kindergarten. There is always a station that is about the current unit of study. In kindergarten at the beginning of the year, you would start with geometry, numbers and counting.

6. **Where should I put them?** Teachers put them where they are comfortable with them. Some teachers have specific spots where each station is to be worked on. Some teachers let students take the workstations where they want to and do the work. It really just depends on the temperament of the teacher. Some teachers state that they want the students to get up and have a brain break after a workstation so they use the rotations for this purpose.

7. **How do students know where to go?** The schedules are important. They should be clear as day so students know where to go and what they are going to do when they get there. I like to use pictures in the schedules with primary students because then they can see themselves up there. I'm like, "That's you so you know where to go." I also like the use of color because then students can learn where to go by looking at the colors; for example, maybe green means to go to the place value center. I encourage people to use digital schedules because then you instantly have a record and you can put the timer up there so students can pace themselves in the workstation. I also think it is a great idea to take pictures of students in action at that workstation and put it up as a picture clue so everyone can see what they are supposed to be doing in that station.

8. **Start small!** Start small and you will eventually do BIG THINGS! Just start!

Made in the USA
Monee, IL
16 April 2021